NO TRAGIC STORY

NO TRAGIC STORY

The Fall of the House of Campbell

RAYMOND CAMPBELL PATERSON

JOHN DONALD

EDINBURGH

Published by John Donald, an imprint of
Birlinn Limited
West Newington House
10 Newington Road
Edinburgh
EH9 1QS

www.birlinn.co.uk

ISBN 0 85976 554 7

British Library Cataloguing-in-Publication Data
A catalogue record for this book is available from the British Library

Typeset by Initial Typesetting Services, Edinburgh
Printed and bound by Cox & Wyman Ltd, Reading, Berkshire

Contents

Tho' my head fall, that is no tragick story,
Since going hence I enter endless glory.

Archibald Campbell, ninth Earl of Argyll

This book is for Nioeka de la Caridad

Foreword

Late in the evening of Saturday 2 May 1685, three ships set sail from Holland. On board the *Anna*, the largest of the vessels, was a small, heavily bearded man who went by the name of 'Mr Carr'.[1] Once the party was safely clear of the coast 'Mr Carr' was revealed, to those not already aware of the deception, as Archibald Campbell, the ninth Earl of Argyll. The little flotilla was making not for Venice or for Surinam in South America, as some of the Dutch soldiers on board appear to have been told,[2] but for Scotland. Argyll was returning home to a country from which he had fled over three years before in fear of his life. In making this dangerous voyage, the Campbell chief, long since condemned as a fugitive and a traitor, had one simple aim in mind: to begin a revolution that would topple the Catholic James VII of Scotland, who had recently succeeded his brother Charles to the throne of Great Britain as James II.

Since the days of King Robert Bruce the Campbell family had built up considerable power in the Highlands and Islands as allies of the royal house against the more unruly elements headed, above all, by the Macdonald Lords of the Isles. The garb of a revolutionary was not one that fitted comfortably on the shoulders of any *MacCailen Mor*; and for the ninth earl, one of the most moderate men of his generation, it was a particularly unusual mode of dress. The seeds of this remarkable transformation were planted earlier in the seventeenth century.

Lacking the resources to pay for a standing army, the Scottish crown had always relied on great families to impose its will in the north. The price of this service often took the form of additional land grants, usually at the expense of those who had incurred the displeasure of the sovereign. Clan Campbell had benefited greatly from this policy, extending its power over most of mainland Argyll and the southern Isles. Successive earls of Argyll had also concentrated judicial and feudal authority in their hands, often used to extend their power still further. Inevitably this caused resentment in those less well placed, or in other noble houses jealous of a rival's success, but there was little anyone could do for as long as the Campbells maintained their axis with the crown. In the late 1630s, during the reign of Charles I, this axis weakened, and then broke.

The decades before the rebellion of 1685 were arguably the most turbulent in Campbell history, in which the family rose to new heights, only to fall to even greater depths. In 1661, for the first time in history, a Campbell chief met his death at the hands of the public executioner. Although the family recovered from this disaster, things were never quite the same again. Like jackals at the gate, the many enemies of the Campbells lay in wait. Lacking the political acumen of his great father, the ninth earl walked into two traps, the first laid by accident and the second by design. By the early 1680s it looked as if the Argyll Campbells were gone forever as a force in Highland politics. Argyll's 1685 invasion was in large measure an attempt to recover from the abyss.

Unlike the Duke of Monmouth's rising of the same year in south-west England, the Argyll rebellion is a largely forgotten episode in Scottish history. There is no surprise in this: Monmouth's rebellion was dramatic in its conception and tragic in its outcome. The Battle of Sedgemoor and the Bloody Assizes are brief but memorable features on the English historical landscape, living on in fiction and romance. Argyll's rebellion, while no less tragic in its consequences, had all the elements of farce, which quickly flared into light and just as quickly fell into dark. Despite the Campbell chief's great expectations and the lavish promises he made to his comrades, it never really took hold. Perhaps the best assessment of its flickering course was provided by the Earl of Perth, who wrote soon after its collapse that 'it really lookt lyke the evanishing of a fantosme, or lyke a thaw. . .'.[3]

Argyll, it also has to be said, was in so many ways the worst kind of man to lead a popular rebellion, lacking all the shallow charm and charisma of Monmouth. Yet, of the two, he was by far the stronger personality, the driving force behind the risings in both England and Scotland. While Monmouth dithered Argyll planned, finally prodding the reluctant duke into action. Argyll's landing in Scotland was intended as the first act in a nationwide rising against King James. Even the failure of the venture was not without significance. Believing he had disposed of his greatest enemies, James acted with increasing arrogance, which led directly to his ruin in 1688. For this, and other reasons, the Argyll rebellion deserves to be rescued from the oblivion to which it has been unjustly consigned.

The task of this book is to place the events of 1685 in the context of Highland history and, more broadly, in the context of Scottish history as a whole. Above all, it explores the process by which the Campbells were transformed from lawmen into rebels, and the impact this had on the politics of the Highlands and the future of the Stewart dynasty itself. For urging me along this particular road my thanks are due to my publisher, Hugh Andrew.

R. C. P.

Edinburgh, 2001

1

Campbells and Covenanters

At the beginning of the seventeenth century the power
and prestige of the Campbell family was close to its
height. Under Archibald Campbell, the seventh Earl of
Argyll, and his son and namesake Archibald, Lord Lorne
– the future eighth earl – the Campbells expanded steadily
at the expense of their Macdonald neighbours. The
Macdonalds of Dunyveg, once the most powerful branch
of the family, went under in 1615, having lost all the
lands they formerly possessed on Kintyre and Islay; at
the outset of his reign in 1625, King Charles I had sanctioned the Campbells' destruction of the Maciains of
Ardnamurchan, one of the smaller branches of Clan
Donald. For a time it even looked as if the Macdonalds
of Clanranald would fall victim to Campbell imperialism.

From Edinburgh and then London the Stewart kings
were always ready to use the house of Argyll as their
chief ally against the lawless clans of the western
Highlands. For the hapless victims there was no appeal
against a family that managed to cloak personal ambition

in the garb of the law. By the late 1630s, however, the picture began to change: the great religious and political crisis that opened in 1637, and peaked the following year with the signing of the National Covenant, broke the age-old link between the Campbells and the Stewarts. For the Macdonalds and the other enemies of the house of Argyll the time of reckoning had come.[1]

James VI and I had bequeathed a dangerous legacy to his son: a belief that sovereigns ruled by the will of God and need not trouble themselves overmuch with human counsel. But while James tempered his folly with a little earthly wisdom, the same cannot be said of Charles. Earlier in the seventeenth century James had skilfully prodded a reluctant Scotland along an Episcopalian road against the Presbyterian inclinations of most of the people. However, he only took the process as far as he thought politically advisable, stopping well short of the high Anglicanism of his southern kingdom. For the Scots, bishops were one thing, but prayer books and ritual, with all the overtones they carried of ancient Catholic practices, quite another. Ignoring the example of his father, Charles decided to press the matter, requiring the Scots to accept a new Anglican-style prayer book, sight unseen, in the summer of 1637. In the process he created a revolution, the greatest political and religious upheaval since the Reformation. In early 1638 the Scots, in a mood of deep anger against royal arrogance, adopted the National Covenant, which bound all signatories to one simple principle: that there should be no innovations in religious practice that had not first been tested by free parliaments and general assemblies of the church. Those who adhered to this document were soon to be called Covenanters. In November 1638 the General Assembly, the first for many years, met in Glasgow. Dominated by Covenanters, it not only declared the king's prayer book illegal but also took the even more dramatic step of abolishing episcopacy itself.[2]

While these events were unfolding Clan Campbell's affairs were under the direction of Archibald Lord Lorne, acting in the place of his father, who had converted to Catholicism some years before and was living in London, estranged from his Protestant kin. Although he was a staunch Protestant, Lorne, as a privy councillor and a member of the Scottish government, remained aloof from the agitation surrounding the National Covenant. This changed with the arrival in Scotland of James, Marquis of Hamilton, appointed by the king to bring an end to the crisis in the north. Instead, he made it worse. It was thanks to him that the Campbells, first among the king's friends, soon became first among his enemies.

Like the Reformation itself, the Covenanter movement made little impact in the western Highlands, especially in those areas under the control of Clan Donald, which remained loyal to the old Catholic faith in opposition to the Protestant Campbells. Although much declined in both power and stature since the days of the Lord of the Isles, the various branches of Clan Donald never lost sight of their ancient heritage. Randal Macdonnell, Earl of Antrim, heading the Irish branch of the family, had ambitions to recover the Dunyveg lands in Kintyre and Islay lost to the Campbells earlier in the century. Realising that matters in Scotland might come to a military show-down, Hamilton attempted to harness both the ambitions of Antrim and the martial energy of Clan Donald in the service of the king.[3] In the process he laid the foundations of a war between the Campbells and Macdonalds, the most bloody in the history of the two clans, which was to be fought with savage intensity between 1644 and 1647.

It is not at all certain that Hamilton, at best a second-rate politician and third-rate schemer, had any clear idea of what he intended to accomplish. As opponents of both the Covenant and the Campbells, Clan Donald would be a formidable ally for the king. But since the fourteenth century the Campbells had been the Stewarts' most reliable Highland supporters, and Lord Lorne had given no indication that he intended to break with his family's traditional loyalties. It may be that Hamilton, aware of Lorne's Presbyterian inclinations, simply intended to ensure that he would make no move contrary to the interests of the king. If so, the strategy was politically inept. Lorne's father, the seventh earl, was still alive and living in London, and could easily be used to undermine the authority of his son. Hamilton simply induced the final breach between the king and the Campbells, ensuring that when the moment was right Lorne, now fully aware of his scheming, would declare for the Covenant. That November, while the General Assembly was in session, Argyll died. Lorne came to Glasgow as a privy councillor; he left as a Covenanter.

Back in Inveraray, the new Earl of Argyll set about strengthening his defences. Kintyre and Islay were both fortified and a number of leading Macdonalds arrested, including Coll Coitach of Colonsay and two of his sons. Alasdair, Coll's other son, managed to escape to Ireland, to the everlasting regret of the Campbells. Antrim, witnessing the continuing misfortunes of his Scottish kin, declared in a mood of impotent frustration that 'until the end of the world no MacDonnell shall enjoy a foot of land in Scotland.'[4]

Unable to solve their differences by diplomatic means the king and the Covenanters went to war in the summer of 1639. The so-called Bishops' Wars of 1639 and 1640 saw little real fighting, but they left the king in an even more desperate position than before. He had ruled England for eleven years without calling parliament; by 1640 he was so short of money that he had little choice but to summon a new assembly. Headed by John Pym, John Hampden and eventually Oliver Cromwell, the Puritan opposition was far more eager to address political and religious grievances in England than the crisis in the north. Charles made the best peace he could with the Covenanters, leaving the new Presbyterian establishment firmly in place, while his political problems in England grew steadily worse. In a desperate search for allies against his troublesome parliament, Charles came to Scotland in 1641 to woo the Covenanters. Argyll, now the leading figure in the government of Scotland, was created a marquis, but this made absolutely no difference to the plight of the king. Scotland remained neutral when Charles and the Puritans went to war in the autumn of 1642.

There were, however, some in Scotland who were concerned by the drift of events. There were particular worries over the growth of Campbell power, now reaching unparalleled heights. In 1640, on the eve of the second Bishops' War, it was reported that Argyll's soldiers were saying that they were not 'King Stewart's but King Campbell's men'. At one point it was even suggested that 'King Campbell' might assume the old Roman office of dictator. James Graham, the fifth Earl of Montrose, one of the first signatories of the National Covenant in 1638, jealous of Argyll and worried for the king, moved steadily away from his former associates, with dramatic and unforeseen consequences.

Randal Macdonnell, Earl of Antrim, never gave up on the hope that he would one day recover the lost Scottish inheritance of his family. A restless intriguer, he embarked on one plot after another. His scheme to invade Scotland during the first Bishops' War had come to nothing; undaunted, he met the king at York in late 1642 and proposed an even grander strategy. In 1641 the general mood of disaffection had spread from mainland Britain to Ireland. Worried by both Covenanters and Puritans, and eager to gain religious concessions from the king, the Catholic Irish rose in revolt, subsequently organising themselves in a confederacy based at Kilkenny. Antrim now proposed a scheme of breathtaking grandeur: Charles, he suggested, should make peace with the Irish Confederates and use them, along with Montrose and the other dissident Scots, in a mighty offensive against his enemies in all three kingdoms. Charles, ignoring the neutrality of Argyll and the Covenanters, and even the intense hostility towards the Catholic Irish among his royalist supporters in England, agreed to this proposal. Neither man seems to have paused to consider that the union of all the king's friends would also mean the union of all the king's enemies.

No more competent than Hamilton as a plotter, the details of Antrim's plan became known in the spring of 1643, when Scots soldiers serving against the Catholic rebels in Ireland captured him. The result was highly predictable. In Scotland, Robert Baillie, a leading minister, expressed the general sense of outrage:

> A commission was given to Antrim to treat with the Irish rebels, that the English and they might agree . . . the first service of the reconciled Ireland and England should be the disposal of the disaffected Scots; that they should goe by sea to Carlile, wher Nithsdale and other Southland lords should joyne; that Colekittoch's sones should waken

our Isles; that McClaine and Gorrum, and the other clanes disaffected to the Campbells, should goe to armes; that Huntly and his son Aboyne, with Bamfe, Airlie, Montrose and the Marshall, should raise our North . . . that so in a trace we should become a field of blood.[5]

Soon the Covenanters abandoned their neutrality and entered into a military and political alliance with the English parliament known as the Solemn League and Covenant. Among other things the English Puritans agreed, or so the Scots were led to believe, that Presbyterianism should be established throughout the United Kingdom. In pursuit of this alliance the Scots army entered England in 1644 and helped inflict a serious defeat on the king's northern army at the Battle of Marston Moor.

Antrim managed to escape from the Scots and went to Oxford, where he met Montrose. Working closely together, both men devised a scheme for a major diversionary attack on the Covenanter government. With the help of the Kilkenny authorities, one of Antrim's plans finally came to fruition: some 1600 soldiers, headed by Alasdair MacColla, Coll Coitach's son, landed in the western Highlands in the summer of 1644. Montrose's own effort to invade Scotland across the western border was, however, a dismal failure; in disguise, and virtually alone, he finally met Alasdair in Atholl in late August, ready to head a crusade against Campbells and Covenanters.

For a year Alasdair and Montrose, now a marquis, enjoyed remarkable success, defeating one army after another, inspiring the Macdonalds and many other anti-Campbell clans by their example. Many joined the loyalists, with an effect just the opposite of the one Montrose intended. Contrary to his hopes and expectations, he was pulled ever deeper into an almost exclusively Highland war. At Tippermuir near Perth and again at Aberdeen he won two quick victories in succession, which he wanted to follow up by a descent on the Lowlands. The Highlanders, in contrast, and particularly the men of Clan Donald, were anxious to begin an attack on the Campbell heartlands. Montrose was presented with a simple choice: go to Argyll or lose your army. It was John Moidertach, the Clanranald chief, who argued that his people

> with all of the clane Donald, have such a mind to revenge the injurie and tyrannous oppression wherewith Ardgyll, more than any of his predecessoures, had insulted over them, resolves that, unlesse the generall make his first worke to enter wpon the Cambelles and the whole countrie of Ardgyll, they would goe no forder on, but would againe retre unto there countrie.[6]

Alasdair at once supported John Moidertach, arguing that 'if McAllanmore could be brought lowe, the whole highlandes wold take armes for the king.' Accepting the inevitable, Montrose led his army into Argyllshire in December 1644. Argyll, wintering in Inveraray, was taken by complete surprise, although he managed to escape down Loch Fyne in his galley before being boxed up in his castle. In the next few weeks the countryside was devastated, and all those capable of bearing arms were killed. The bloodletting had little to do with either Covenants or kings; this was a feud with deep roots in history. Father James MacBreck, the Catholic priest who accompanied the Highlanders and Irish, emphasised the crusading element in his subsequent report.

> The Catholic regiments, however, and their leader Alexander Macdonald, longed earnestly to fight it out

with the Campbells, who had long been their fiercest persecutors and, whenever they could, the murderers and assassins of Catholics, in the north of Ireland and the whole of Scotland. The entire conduct of the war, and the whole hazard of their cause, turned upon this simple point, and they considered that they would effect nothing worthy of their efforts unless they crushed the Campbells, devastated Argyll with fire and sword, and administered a terrible and telling chastisement to this hideous receptacle of bandits, plunderers, incendiaries and cut-throats.[7]

For the once-invincible Campbells this was bad enough; worse was to follow. After the Highland army withdrew they made a quick recovery: Argyll returned from the south with some Lowland soldiers, and the Campbell soldiers returned from service in Ireland. Montrose was advancing up the Great Glen in the direction of Inverness when he learned that the Campbells were collecting to his rear, by the old fortress of Inverlochy in Lochaber. He turned back, though not by the direct route, arriving on the enemy flank in early February 1645. In the ensuing battle the Campbells suffered the most serious defeat in their history, observed by Argyll from the safety of his galley on Loch Linnhe. After so many years of humiliation and retreat the Macdonalds had their revenge, celebrated in verse by Iain Lom, the Bard of Keppoch.

Early on Sunday morning I climbed the brae above the Castle of Inverlochy, I saw the army arraigning for battle, And victory in the field was with Clan Donald . . .

The most pleasing news every time it was announced About the wry-mouthed Campbells, was that every company Of them as they came along had their heads battered with Sword blows.

9

Were you not familiar with the Goirtean Odhar? Well was
It manured, not with the dung of sheep or goats, but by the
Blood of Campbells after it congealed.

Perdition take you if I feel pity for your plight, as I
Listen to the distress of your children, lamenting the
    company
Which was in the battlefield, the wailing of the women
Of Argyll.[8]

For a time it looked as if the whole political landscape of
Scotland might be changed: that the Campbells would
lose their ancient power in the Highlands forever and
that the Covenanters would be overwhelmed. In August
1645, the last Covenanter army in Scotland was defeated
at Kilsyth near Glasgow, forcing Argyll to flee across the
border to Berwick-upon-Tweed for his own safety. In
London, his kinsman John Campbell, Earl of Loudon,
made a tearful appeal to the English parliament for
assistance, a sad reversal of the position of only two years
before. But in the end the triumphs of the royalists came
to nothing, for the simple reason that Alasdair and
Montrose were fighting entirely different wars. Montrose
wanted to defeat the Covenanters prior to advancing to
the aid of the king, now steadily losing his war against
the puritans in England. Alasdair and the rest of Clan
Donald were less ambitious: they were fighting to ensure
that the Campbells would never recover from the blow
they had received at Inverlochy. In August 1645 the two
commanders parted, never to meet again. Montrose
advanced to the borders and his catastrophic defeat at
Philiphaugh at the hands of Scottish soldiers detached
from the army in England; Alasdair returned to
Argyllshire, with the approval of Antrim, to continue his
tribal war against Clan Campbell.

For almost two years Alasdair and his allies dominated the Campbell heartlands in Argyllshire, and Antrim crossed from Ireland in the summer of 1646 to lay claim to his ancient patrimony, an event celebrated in verse by an anonymous poet.

Welcome to Scotland to the Marquis and his army
As they march with martial strains to the land of his
Ancestors, the regal people that were lordly.
Macdonalds of Isla were they, and kings of the Isles
Of heroes. May sovereignty over land and sea be to
The royal company of the banners . . .

Every deceiver will get what he deserves, and
Every traitor will be laid low. We will not have
A yoke to bear, and offenders will not have their
Will. The people of the wrymouths [Campbells]   will
   be trampled
Under our heels, and Clan Donald will be on top, as was
Usual for that people.[9]

Despite all these exaggerated expectations, Antrim did not remain for long. These events in Argyllshire, dramatic as they were, were little more than a sideshow to the main drama being acted out far to the south. Charles was defeated by the recently created New Model Army, commanded by Sir Thomas Fairfax and Oliver Cromwell. With no further function, the main Scots army returned from England in 1647. Alasdair did his best to defend himself in Kintyre, but with his enemies concentrating against him he fled back to Ireland, where he was killed later that year, while Argyll returned to Inveraray.

His obvious incompetence as a soldier, and the successive defeats of his clan, had weakened some of the

Campbell chief's prestige; but he was still a well-respected figure, especially among the more radical sections of the Covenanter movement, soon to be known as the Kirk Party. His views were not shared by most of his fellow peers, who, worried by the continuing crisis in England, broke from the radicals and formed an alliance with Charles, now a prisoner on the Isle of Wight, who agreed to establish Presbyterianism in England for a three-year trial period. Under this treaty, known as the Engagement, a Scots army entered England against the wishes of Argyll and the Kirk Party, opposed to any compromise on the pure principle of the Covenants. Under the command of Hamilton, even less competent as a soldier than as a politician, the army marched to disaster. No sooner were the Engagers defeated by Cromwell at the Battle of Preston than the Covenanter communities of south-west Scotland rose in revolt and advanced on Edinburgh, an episode famous in Scottish history as the Whiggamore Raid. The term 'whiggam' was apparently used in Ayrshire and Galloway by people urging on their horses. In time it gave rise to the word 'Whig', used to describe extreme Covenanters.

The Covenanters consolidated their hold on the government of Scotland with the aid of Cromwell, who came to Edinburgh and conferred with Argyll at Moray House, where the two men seemed to have established a good understanding. Nevertheless, neither Argyll nor any other member of the Kirk Party approved what followed. Ignoring the protests of the Scots, the Puritans put Charles on trial and executed him in January 1649. It was a particularly serious blow to Argyll, who, following from his recent conversations with Cromwell, had hoped to continue to influence affairs throughout the United Kingdom. Caught between the English republicans, on the one hand, and the more extreme Covenanters on the other, his power soon began to evaporate. Years later, while awaiting his own execution, he expressed his feelings in a little book written for his eldest son Archibald, Lord Lorne.

> By that confusion my thoughts became distracted and myself encountered so many difficulties in the way, that all remedies that were applied had quite the contrary operation; whatever, therefore hath been said by me or others in this matter, you must repute and accept them as from a distracted man of a distracted subject in a distracted time wherein I lived.[10]

Soon after the execution of Charles I, his son was proclaimed as King Charles II in Edinburgh. Among the first to write to the new king expressing his unqualified loyalty was Lord Lorne. In this, the first act in his public life, he openly displayed himself as a royalist, who, if necessary, would even serve against his own father.[11] In general, Lorne seems to have shared few of his father's convictions, and appears never to have been ideologically committed in any deep sense to the Covenants: religion was to play little part in determining his outlook on life, at least not until his last few years.

Charles was allowed to come over to Scotland from Holland in the summer of 1650, but only after he agreed to sign the Covenants and, against his judgement and conscience, impose Presbyterianism throughout his three kingdoms. His experience at the hands of the Covenanter preachers left him with an abiding hatred of all strictness in religion. Even Argyll, firm in his own religious observance, was moved to sympathise with the plight of the young king, subject to endless sermonising. His son, Lord Lorne, certainly showed Charles every consideration; when he was appointed colonel in the king's lifeguards he insisted that the commission should be granted by Charles, although for some time past these military appointments were subject to parliamentary approval only.[12] In time to come Charles was never to express anything but satisfaction with Lorne's conduct, and there is certainly no basis for Clarendon's accusation that he treated the king with 'rudeness and barbarity'.[13] Charles could be magnanimous and generous, but he never forgot personal injury.

The arrival of Charles in Scotland was a clear threat to English security. It was followed, almost immediately, by the invasion of Cromwell. After some prolonged military manoeuvring, the Covenanters were finally defeated at Dunbar on 3 September, arguably one of the most unnecessary battles in Scottish history. Serving in the lifeguards, Lorne had his first experience of the bitterness of defeat, which was to be such a feature of his life as a soldier. On the other side of the field was a young lieutenant in Cromwell's New Model Army by the name of Richard Rumbold. Neither man knew the other; but by the strange workings of fate they were destined to have a close future acquaintance.

The defeat at Dunbar weakened the hold of the Kirk Party, which continued the process of sectarian subdivision, fragmenting into extreme and moderate factions known as Protesters and Resolutioners. Argyll, in the last major act of his public life, placed the crown on the head of the king at Scone on New Year's Day 1651. Soon after his power, which had been waning for some time, faded away altogether. Charles, at last allowed to act with all the powers of a king, raised a new army and made ready to invade England, ignoring Argyll's opposition to the plan. The marquis, now little regarded, returned to

Inveraray, while Charles marched to defeat at Worcester. We have no firm evidence of Lord Lorne's whereabouts at this time, although it seems most likely that he returned with his father to Argyllshire. Evading his enemies, the king escaped back to the continent while the English completed the conquest of Scotland. Argyll, bending to the inevitable, made his own peace with the enemy in 1652. His remarkable public career, which kept him at the centre of affairs for over ten years, was now over. As a legacy, however, he was crushed by debt and burdened with many enemies, not least of whom was Charles himself.

The years that followed were some of the most difficult in Campbell history. Forced on occasion to hide from his creditors in Inveraray, Argyll was also troubled by growing political and personal differences between Lord Lorne and himself. Remaining true to his royalist convictions, and against the express wishes of his father, Lorne was one of the first to join the 1653 revolt against the English, known after its first commander as the Glencairn Rising. Argyll, aware of the difficulties his son's actions would place him in, wrote to Lorne in a clear mood of impotent desperation: 'And let all the curse and judgements in God's word against disobedient children to parents come upon you and pursue you til they overtake you, and let nothing you take in hand prosper, for you are a crosse (I may say a curse) to your father and heaviness to your mother, if you continue in your waies.'[14]

True to his promise to the king, Lorne simply ignored his father. It was reported to Charles by Sir Robert Moray that Argyll would oppose the rising for the sake of self-preservation, but Lord Lorne was a determined loyalist. 'As your Majesty will find by his letters, hath ever been without the merest shadow of compliance of any kind most invincibly constant and faithful to your Majesty's service and interest, and will most fully, heartily and actively joyne with those that appear here for your Majesty, as they all know, should it cost him all he values most on earth.'[15]

His presence was less than welcome to some of his fellow royalists, however, particularly Angus Macdonald, the Glengarry chief, who had fought with Alasdair and Montrose at Inverlochy and showed every sign of wishing to turn the rising into yet another anti-Campbell crusade.[16] Glencairn himself is said to have distrusted Lorne, who was soon expressing grave doubts about the abilities of his commander. Lorne's participation in the rising placed Argyll himself under suspicion, but it was soon clear to the occupying authorities that he had little real influence over his rebel clansmen. At one point he was even forced to make an ignominious appeal for English troops to save him from the violence of his own son.

Torn by rivalry, and badly led, the Glencairn Rising flickered and died. Interestingly, in this regard at least, it resembles Argyll's own rising in 1685. Even the arrival from the continent of General John Middleton, Charles' leading Scottish officer, did little to revive its fortunes. With the approval of Middleton, Lorne made his own peace with the English in May 1655. He also made his peace with his father, although the rift between them was never completely healed. Despite his submission, Lorne was never entirely trusted by the occupying authorities, headed by General George Monck. In 1657, he refused to take an oath denouncing the Stewarts and approving Cromwell's Protectorate. He was arrested, spending some time as a prisoner in Edinburgh Castle prior to the Restoration of the king in 1660.

After the barren years of Cromwell's military dictatorship, and the political uncertainty that followed his death in 1658, the Restoration was widely welcomed as a joyful occasion. It was, however, also a time of reckoning. For the Campbells the bill was to be particularly high.

2

A time of suffering

Lord Lorne was among the first to attend the king in Whitehall. As a proven royalist he was well received by Charles, who appears to have given him the impression that his father would also be welcomed.[1] Others were not so sure. On the day Charles arrived in England, Robert Baillie's daughter and son-in-law were at Rosneath, one of the marquis' homes, and reported 'all the dogs that day did take a strange yowling and glowring up at My Lord's chamber windows for some houres together.'[2]

Against the advice of at least some of his friends, Argyll arrived in London in July 1660, seeking an interview with Charles. Instead he was promptly arrested and imprisoned in the Tower, where he remained for the next five months, before being sent back to Edinburgh in December to stand trial on a charge of treason. Argyll, whose crimes were no greater than many others, was effectively selected to serve as a sacrificial goat for past disorders. His many enemies, headed above all by John, Earl of Middleton,

Charles' High Commissioner to the Scottish parliament, were clearly determined that the Restoration would see a new beginning, and that the power of the Campbells would never be allowed to revive. In the trial, which opened in early 1661, Argyll faced a variety of charges, including complicity in the murder of Charles I. Of this Gilbert Burnet later wrote: 'The Earl of Middleton resolved, if possible, to have the king's death fastened on him. By this means, as he would die with the more infamy, so he reckoned this would put an end to the family, since nobody durst move in favour of the son of one judged guilty of that crime. And he, as believed, hoped to obtain a grant of his estate.'[3]

Argyll answered all accusations against him with great skill, and, despite Middleton's best efforts, was acquitted of any responsibility for the death of Charles. As for the charge that he unlawfully made war on the sovereign, this was effectively covered by the 1651 Act of Indemnity, which, if set aside, would have placed almost all of the Scottish nobility in the dock, including Middleton himself. In the end it looked as if the prosecution's case, prepared with great care, would fall completely. At virtually the last moment a number of letters were sent to Edinburgh by George Monck, the last Cromwellian commander in Scotland, which proved that Argyll had collaborated with the English authorities during the Glencairn Rising.[4] Monck was a cautious individual, highly unlikely to have taken this action without the active encouragement of the king.[5] Argyll was duly condemned as a traitor and beheaded on Monday, 27 May 1661 by the Maiden, a primitive Scottish guillotine. In a poem supposedly written to celebrate the coronation of the king, Iain Lom, the Bard of Keppoch, anticipated the death of the Campbell chief with a fierce joy.

Dire is the lesson – unless, O God, Thou dost succour
him that awaits the merciless Earl on Wednesday.

When his collar is torn off, his head will be severed from
his body – all glory and praise to the King on high.

By the sharp austere maiden that leaves jaws powerless,
and will close forever the malevolent Marquis's squint.

Although it is the beginning it is not the end for those
who set the fire alight. May the rest of his friends fare as
    I wish.

Just like the plight of Lucifer of a time-after being an
Angel at first, he was mercilessly ejected from Paradise:

So will you now roam as a demon throughout the world,
an accomplice of his, according to all appearances . . .[6]

While the trial was underway, Lorne had remained in
London attempting to intercede for his father. Nothing
availed. Lorne learned of his father's death from his
kinsman the Earl of Loudon, who wrote soon after, 'God
was gracious to him, in clearing him from the most
heinous crimes, and giving him strength to die with much
Cristian courage and patience.'[7]

Middleton had achieved part of his aim. Lord Lorne,
who, as the son of a forfeited traitor, was not allowed to
succeed to his father's titles and estates, was soon to enter
one of the most dangerous phases of his life.

Having removed the Covenanter Marquis, Middleton,
who had converted from Presbyterianism to Episco-
palianism during his exile, set about restoring the old
order in religion and politics prior to the revolution. In
London, John Maitland, second Earl and subsequently
Duke of Lauderdale, Charles' Secretary of State for
Scotland and formerly a leading Covenanter, urged a

moderate Presbyterian settlement in the north; but this sensible advice was simply ignored. In cleansing the Augean Stables, Middleton had an Act Recissory passed by parliament, wiping out all public legislation right back to 1633. This included, among other things, the Presbyterian constitution of the Kirk. With breakneck speed, and against the inclination of the more cautious king, Episcopacy was put back in place, as was the right of landlords to appoint ministers to livings under their control, a practice that had been abolished during the high noon of the Covenant. James Sharp, created Archbishop of St Andrews, was appointed to head the new Episcopal establishment. Sharp, a talented if self-serving individual, had been a leading Presbyterian minister, and his perceived treason was deeply resented by his less pragmatic colleagues. Many ministers, particularly in the south-west of Scotland, where the covenanting tradition had taken deep roots, refused to accept the new powers of the bishops and landlords. Soon a great many parishes were abandoned by men like John Blackadder, John Welsh, Donald Cargill and Andrew Peden, who acquired an almost legendary reputation preaching throughout the hillsides of southern Scotland to illegal field assemblies known as conventicles. Middleton was thus the chief architect of the religious troubles that were to become the dominant feature of Restoration Scotland.

Middleton's ambitions were personal, as well as political. He had no territorial power in his own right, so he hoped to gain the lucrative Campbell inheritance. Although Lord Lorne had served under him during the Glencairn Rising, and had earned his praise, Middleton was eager to ensure that he would never receive his lost inheritance. According to James Kirkton, the historian of the Presbyterian Church, Middleton hoped, in time, to become Duke of Argyll.[8] To achieve this Lorne would first have to be destroyed.

After the death of his father, Lord Lorne stayed in London attempting to revive the fortunes of his family, with limited success.[9] In July 1661 the king was reminded of the age-old role the Campbells had played in Highland politics in a letter written by Lorne and his chief cadets. The letter records the loyalty of the successive Campbell chiefs in opposing rebels back to the days of Somerled, the progenitor of Clan Donald.

> Many horrid insurrections and rebellions of Islanders, and remote mountaneous men that have been broken, destroyed and overthrown by our Cheiffs and ther freinds, and how many notorious malefactors and cruell oppressors have been brought from ther strong holds and inaccessible places, otherways hardly to be overtaken without great blood shead and expence, and yet have been overcome and brought by our Cheifs to ther condigne punishment . . . never have any of our cheifs, of the house of Argyll or other Cousings or Cadeitts have been tainted to this day with the least mark of disloyalty or disobedience to ther soveraign lords, the kings of Scotland . . .[10]

Although the king, who had commended Lorne for his loyalty on several occasions, was sympathetic, his enemies at court were active in preventing any sympathetic treatment of the son of a traitor. Aware of the opposition he faced, Lorne wrote to the Earl of Lothian.

> All endevoures are used by some heere to prevent or render ineffectual his Majestie's favour to me, but I am confident, upon what he expresses every day, that it shall not be in ther power to obstruct it. In the meane time, some insult, and others despaire and are carried away

with the speate. The Lord in all this is to be waited on,
who knows how unjustly some pursue me.[11]

Despite his mood of optimism, however, there were
points when Lorne seemed close to being overwhelmed
by the malice of his enemies. On one occasion he
apparently considered leaving for Jamaica to begin life
anew as a planter.[12] Instead he persisted in his efforts to
have the Argyll estates restored, in the process walking
straight into a trap.

The chief obstruction Lorne faced at court was from
Edward Hyde, Earl of Clarendon, Charles' chief minister
and an ally of Middleton. Thomas Howard, Lord
Berkshire, a friend of Clarendon's, promised that he
would try to win him over provided Lorne paid £1000
for the service. Trusting in this shady deal, Lord Lorne
wrote to Lord Duffus, his brother-in-law, saying of his
enemies in the Scottish parliament that the 'king will see
their tricks'.[13] On its way to Scotland this letter was intercepted and brought before Middleton. Acting at once,
Middleton submitted the document to parliament, which
agreed that Lorne's remark was a gross reflection on its
conduct, and that he should be charged with 'leasing-
making' – sowing dissension between the king and his
subjects – a capital crime. When the matter was put to
Charles he took the view that Lorne's remark was
indiscreet rather than criminal, but bowed to the will of
parliament, which had given many proofs of its loyalty.
Charles was never averse to abandoning even his closest
advisors when his own interests were at stake. In sending
Lorne to Edinburgh to stand trial, he at least instructed
Middleton that any sentence passed was to be referred
back to him.[14]

Lorne arrived in Edinburgh in July 1662 and was
immediately placed in close confinement in the castle,

for the second time in his life. It was just over a year since the death of his father, and some were moved to write that the ancient house of Argyll had reached an especially low point in its fortunes.[15] Alexander Brodie, one of Lorne's friends, confined his own feelings to his diary, remarking on the obvious injustice of the whole procedure: 'It's observabl[e] how much he suffered for the King by the usurpers; the danger that his lyf was in by them; and how he suffers by the King's authoritie. This is a providence not to be neglected.'[16]

When he appeared before the court, Lorne made no defence, only saying in mitigation that he had acted under great provocation in the face of the many false accusations that had been made against him: 'Some of these had been put in the king's own hands, to represent him as unworthy of his grace and favour: so, after all that hard usage, it was no wonder that he wrote with some sharpness: but he protested that he meant no harm to any person; his design being only to preserve and save himself from the malice and lies of others.'[17]

His plea was simply ignored. On 25 August Lorne knelt before parliament to hear sentence of death pronounced against him.[18] Although the king had instructed that the execution was not to be carried out, there were many in both England and Scotland shocked that what was no more than a passing remark should carry such savage consequences. Even the Earl of Clarendon, no friend of the Campbells, was moved to remark that he gave thanks to God that he did not live in a country where there were such laws. Gilbert Burnet was later to write that the sentence left to posterity the precedent of a parliamentary judgement, which allowed a man to be condemned for a letter of common news.[19]

On the whim of the king, Lorne's life was safe; but he remained imprisoned in Edinburgh Castle for almost a year. At this trying time he was fortunate in one thing: he enjoyed the friendship of Lauderdale, soon to be the dominant political figure of the age. In his youth, Lauderdale had been a leading supporter of the Covenanter regime in Scotland, and, as we have said, favoured a moderate Presbyterian settlement at the Restoration. But above all he was a survivor, never allowing principle to stand in the way of self-interest. Middleton now saw in him a great political rival, and set about laying the kind of traps that brought Lorne close to destruction. But Lorne, who lacked the political skill and intellectual subtlety of his great father, had been a relatively easy target. Lauderdale was altogether different, enjoying the ear and the confidence of the king. In attempting to encompass Lauderdale's downfall, Middleton brought about his own.

Believing himself to be unassailable, Middleton began to act with increasing arrogance. Shortly after Lorne's trial an act was passed by parliament, clearly aimed at Lauderdale, which made it a criminal offence to petition the king on behalf of the children of traitors, even though this was a direct challenge to the royal prerogative of mercy. Having encompassed the extinction of the Campbells, Middleton now moved directly against Lauderdale. Suspecting the Secretary of State of lingering Presbyterian sympathies, he introduced a measure in September, obliging all office holders to denounce the Covenants of 1638 and 1643. Lauderdale was not to be caught so simply, apparently declaring that he could cope with a cartload of such oaths and happily turn Turk rather than lose office.[20] Having failed in this, Middleton proceeded into more dangerous territory.

With the consent of the king, parliament passed an Act of Indemnity, allowing for fines and other penalties against former members of the Kirk Party and collaborators with the Cromwellian regime. In addition, Middleton persuaded parliament to adopt a supplementary measure, disabling twelve as yet unnamed individuals from holding public office for life. These names were to be chosen by secret ballot, but Middleton made sure that Lauderdale was included. Despite his enemies' best efforts, Lauderdale learned of the scheme before the matter was put to the king. Charles had always assumed that only discredited politicians would be ostracised in this fashion, not his own servants. When Lauderdale told him of the true purpose, Charles, always jealous of his own royal privileges, reacted with anger, throwing the Act aside when it was finally presented to him. Middleton was disgraced and removed from office. In the wake of this Lord Lorne was released from prison and the sentence of death against him formally rescinded by parliament;[21] soon after he was created ninth Earl of Argyll. The title of marquis was to remain permanently forfeit.

The following year Argyll was admitted to the Privy Council, and was soon exercising the traditional role of his family in attempting to maintain law and order in the Highlands, acting as the ally of Lauderdale. But he was never to be at the centre of the political stage in the way that his father had been; it's true that he lacked the ability and conviction that drove his father, but virtually by necessity his ambitions were more personal than public. More seriously, the terms of his restoration were to be quite disastrous for the future peace of the Highlands.

Earlier in the century the Marquis of Argyll had, for his services to the Covenanter regime, been awarded estates forfeited by the royalist Marquis of Huntly. Aware that his fortunes might easily change, Argyll set out to strengthen his hold on these lands by buying up all Huntly's debts, giving the creditors the right to seek payment from him. In practice, all this meant was that these unfortunate individuals could line up behind another door forever locked. However, when the Huntly estates were restored to their rightful owners in 1661, the debts were not. When Lorne was restored to his father's property in 1663 he was also deemed liable for all the Huntly debts, although he no longer had the revenues to pay them off. In effect, he was financially ruined. We cannot be sure who was responsible for this one-sided arrangement. Lauderdale, it seems certain, would have preferred Argyll to be restored to all his father's estates, titles and honours. It may be that Charles, acting on the advice of Clarendon, presumably urged on by Huntly himself, agreed to inflict this financial penalty on Argyll to mollify the many enemies of the Campbells.

Pursued by his many creditors, Argyll had little choice but to pursue his debtors, chief among whom were the Macleans of Duart. If Argyll already had too many enemies, his struggle with the Macleans was destined to give him even more. During the civil wars, the Macleans had been consistently loyal to the king, suffering severe losses in his service at the Battle of Inverkeithing in 1651, when the then chief and many of the clan gentry were wiped out. Argyll's war with the Macleans, which was to reach a peak in the late 1670s, recreated the kind of alliance that brought his family close to ruin at the time of Montrose and MacColla. The greatest accusation that can be lodged against him is that he was insufficiently attentive to his plight, which did much to contribute to his second fall from grace in 1681.

Middleton was gone, and Argyll was reasonably safe for as long as he enjoyed the confidence of Lauderdale. Nevertheless, his position was far from secure, and despite his proven loyalty, he was in many ways in a far weaker position than many of his ancestors. Sometime between 1661 and 1663 an anonymous pamphlet circulated warning against his restoration.

> The restoring of this family is in a special manner most dangerous, by reason of the situation and vast bounds of the estate of Argyle in the Highlands, the great claim, many vassals and tenants that depend on it, all, or for the much greater part, ill principled, and inured to rebellion these last 20 years, who blindly follow their master's commands, without any regard to their duty to God or the king, so that it is a most fit place to be a nest and seminary of rebellion, as it proved to be in the late Argyle's time.[22]

It was particularly dangerous to restore Lorne, the author continues, for the vice of rebellion was in his blood. Not only did he support his father's Covenanter principles, but his return to the Highlands would also strengthen the king's enemies and weaken his friends. Argyll was well aware that he had many enemies, both personal and political. In his correspondence with Lauderdale he makes repeated references to the undercurrent of complaint and criticism made against him, remarking in February 1665 'it is cleare what paines some take to misconstrue every thing I doe . . . It hath of late beene told me by some, betwixt jest and earnest, that in endeavouring the peace of the Highlands, I secure my own interest . . .'[23]

Lauderdale himself was in part responsible for Argyll's problems. From the late 1660s onwards there were two strands to the Secretary's policy: to turn Scotland into a secure base for royal absolutism and to settle the religious question bequeathed to him by Middleton. This was to absorb all of his energies, and he never showed that much interest in the politics of the north-west Highlands, content to leave matters in the hands of Argyll. It is also important to bear in mind that Restoration government was essentially government on the cheap. During the Commonwealth and Protectorate the old feudal system, which had operated to the great benefit of the Campbells, had been largely set aside, replaced by a fairer, more objective administration. But this had required time, patience, soldiers and forts. Above all, it required money – lots of money. After 1660, when the last vestiges of the military dictatorship were swept aside, all that remained was a return to traditional solutions to old problems for a government not prepared to waste any more resources in the north. Only Argyll, with a powerful base of support within Clan Campbell, could fill the vacuum left in the west Highlands. The problem with this was that no matter how much he protested, Argyll's public duties inevitably gave all the appearance of personal ambition, which had a seriously destabilising effect in the north. It also outraged the many loyalists whose families had not been sullied by the crime of treason. Argyll was really only safe for as long as Lauderdale was able to shield him from his enemies. This arrangement clearly was not going to last forever.

There were many who also continued to believe that Argyll sympathised with his father's Presbyterian views, including James Sharp, Archbishop of St Andrews, although he never gave them any cause to do so.[24] We find little clue in these years to Argyll's true views on religion. It seems certain though that, like Lauderdale, he would have preferred a moderate Presbyterian settlement, and showed little of the persecuting tendencies of some of his fellow peers and privy councillors.

The religious legacy left by Middleton continued to trouble Scotland in the years after his departure. Faced with the growing problem of field assemblies the government in Scotland, headed by the Earl of Rothes, who had replaced Middleton as High Commissioner to parliament, resorted to outright military repression, a policy supported by the leading clerics, including the archbishops of Glasgow and St Andrews. A backlash was not long in following when, in November 1666, several hundred men in south-west Scotland rose in arms and marched on Edinburgh, under the leadership of James Wallace, who had once served as lieutenant-colonel under Lorne in the king's lifeguards in 1650.

To prove his loyalty, Argyll raised some 1500 men to help deal with the emergency, although they were never called on because Archbishop Sharp is said to have believed that they would only have aided the insurgents.[25] Argyll did, however, remain in arms, taking steps to ensure that the insurrection would not spread to his own lands in southern Kintyre, where some years before his father had established a Lowland plantation to replenish the local communities, depleted by famine and war. Even so, these people do not seem to have been too badly handled and were to be of some service to Argyll when he came back this way under very different circumstances in 1685. The crisis passed just as quickly as it had arisen, when the rebels were defeated in late November at the Battle of Rullion Green in the Pentland Hills.

Despite his best efforts, Argyll once again seems to have been under suspicion at this time. Attempts appear to have been made to gather information against him, and at least one spy is thought to have been operating in Kintyre. In June 1667, Argyll – clearly worried that some false accusations might be made against him – wrote to Lauderdale urging him to trust nothing but what could be proved.[26] All that can really be said is that Kintyre, earlier described by Rothes as a 'nest of thiefs', was remarkably free of the repression that disfigured the southern Lowlands during the Restoration, and seems to have acted as a magnet for those escaping persecution elsewhere.[27] The local register of congregations records that the number of Lowland names in the area doubled between 1665 and 1685, an influx that appears to have placed a considerable strain on local resources.[28]

In the aftermath of the Pentland Rising there was a fundamental change in the government of Scotland. In 1669 Lauderdale came north to replace the discredited Rothes, becoming High Commissioner as well as Secretary of State. As the policy of repression had been a clear failure, Lauderdale decided, with the approval of the king, on a fundamental shift of emphasis, which involved the temporary disgrace of James Sharp. Soon after an Act of Indulgence was introduced, which allowed a limited restoration of some of the less intransigent Presbyterian ministers. This was combined with continuing action against illegal field assemblies, although this problem proved to be particularly intractable. In years to come Lauderdale, in his attempts to stamp these out, and gripped by an increasing mood of frustration, was to adopt measures just as oppressive as those used by Rothes and Sharp.

Parliament opened in October 1669, the first to be presided over by Lauderdale as High Commissioner. It was also the first time in some years that Argyll's creditors and enemies had a chance to act in concert. One of the acts to be passed concerned the formal ratification of Argyll's 1663 restoration. Lauderdale, aware of the strong undercurrent of opposition to this, overruled all debate and refused to put the matter to a vote, saying that it concerned none but the king.[29] Even John Hay, the Earl of Tweeddale, one of Lauderdale's chief allies, was bold enough to say that he was wrong to maintain Argyll against so much opposition, which only led to his own fall from power.[30] But the debt question was simply one that refused to go away, especially as Argyll, ruthless in the pursuit of his creditors, continued to resist the just demands of those to whom he owed money. Even one of his friends, alarmed by a request for a loan, was moved to remark that he was 'noe good debtour', a judgement confirmed by Argyll's own declaration at Campbeltown in 1685.[31]

Soon after the 1669 parliament Argyll, with the backing of the law, decided to force a showdown with the Macleans of Duart. This family, once serious rivals to the Campbells, had been in steady decline since 1600. Even before the outbreak of the civil wars they were in serious financial difficulties, and by 1650 Sir Hector Maclean of Duart admitted to owing the Marquis of Argyll £60 000 Scots.[32] By the 1660s this had risen to a staggering £200 000. With other creditors, and an annual income of little more than £1000, the Macleans could hardly afford to pay the interest, to say nothing of the principal sum. Argyll, therefore, made ready to claim their lands in Morvern, Mull and Tiree. In 1667, Sir Alan Maclean came to London to appeal the king, perhaps hoping to remind him of his clan's sacrifice at Inverkeithing, but Lauderdale successfully blocked his access to the royal presence. In 1674, Argyll decided to take forcible possession of the Maclean lands, and duly obtained a commission of fire and sword from the government, providing him with the authority to do so. A large invasion force was assembled, and the Campbells and their allies landed on Mull, taking Duart Castle in September. Soon after, the Maclean gentry submitted, promising to recognise the authority of Argyll. So far matters had gone reasonably well; but this was only the opening act of a drama that was to last for some five years.

Relishing their long tradition of independence, the Macleans threw off their Campbell yoke in 1675, although in the struggle to come Duart Castle remained in the hands of the enemy. Many Highland chiefs, worried by Campbell expansionism, came to their aid, not least of whom was Angus of Glengarry, created Lord Macdonnell and Aros at the Restoration, who had almost come to blows with Lorne during the Glencairn Rising. Lord Macdonnell, who had pretensions to the chieftain-ship of all Clan Donald, managed to obtain the support of the Macdonalds of Keppoch and Glencoe in this new war with their ancient enemy. Iain Lom also took up the cause, once again wielding his acidy pen in 'A Song to Maclean of Duart'.

It will be a piece with the changing fortune of your Cause, if it is the [Campbell] boar that presses on you as a Threat, that the infection of leprosy should enter into his Vitals.

The sharp stroke of short pens protects Argyll, he who Is as eloquent in conversation as a parrot.

By falsehood you deprived us of Islay green and lovely, And Kintyre with its verdant plains . . .[33]

Even with the support of some regular troops, Argyll was unable to enforce his authority, and an attempted invasion of Mull in 1675 was beaten back by a storm, allegedly raised by a witch.[34]

In forcing this issue, even some of Argyll's friends were sensitive to the dangers he was creating. John Campbell of Glenorchy, his chief kinsman and the future first Earl of Breadalbane, urged caution and moderation, which only incurred resentment. Argyll, as John Lauder of Fountainhall noted, did all according to law, but 'his ambitious grasping at the mastery of the Hylands and Western Ilands of Mull, Ila etc., stirred up the Earl of Seaforth, Marquis of Atholl, Lord Macdonald, Glengarry, Mcloud and other clans into a combination for bearing him doune . . .'[35]

Opposition to Argyll even went as high as the Privy Council. On one occasion he came close to fighting a duel with John Murray, Marquis of Atholl, a long-standing opponent.[36] Unable to obtain support from his colleagues, Argyll went to London to appeal to Lauderdale. So long tied up in his own affairs, which he pursued with a single-minded determination, Argyll's self-righteous conviction of the justice of his cause blinded him to wider political realities. His war with the Macleans brought the kind of disorder to the Highlands that he was supposed to prevent. More seriously he ignored the big picture at a time when the religious troubles in southern Scotland were becoming critical. He was saved, in part, by a storm that was beginning to blow up in southern England. For Catholicism, and the question of who should succeed Charles to the throne, had moved to the centre of the stage, with dramatic consequences.

3

Shall a Catholic be king?

While Argyll continued his war with the Macleans, Lauderdale's quest for a solution to the religious problems of southern Scotland was as far off as ever. The first Indulgence of 1669 was followed by a second in 1672, which further increased the number of Presbyterian parishes. But the policy failed to work in the way that the Secretary intended. In time both of these measures introduced a serious split in the Covenanter underground, separating the moderates from the extremists, as Lauderdale had hoped; but it failed to have the short-term results he desired. Conventicles continued to grow in size, to the point where small armies of radicals could gather in the fields in open defiance of the authorities. In a very real sense it was becoming a problem of public order rather than one of religious dissent, especially as the more radical elements were denouncing the royal government and were openly bearing arms.

Lauderdale, soon aware of the limited impact of the first Indulgence, turned to more extreme measures. In the session of 1670, attempting to control the spread of conventicles, parliament passed the so-called Clanking Act. This was by far the most serious measure passed against dissidents to date: those attending illegal assemblies were to be subject to heavy fines, while rebel ministers were threatened with death. Lauderdale, in effect, was offering his old religious allies a stark and brutal choice: the olive branch of the Indulgence or the club of the Clanking Act.

For the saints of the Covenant, the Secretary's threats were no more regarded than his promises. Conventicles grew at an alarming rate, and to an alarming size. Huge gatherings were held throughout the Lowlands, both in the east and west. In the summer of 1678, no fewer than 14 000 people came to hear Blackadder and Welsh preach at Skeoch Hill in Dumfries-shire. With such large numbers of people wandering the countryside, many bearing arms, a new rebellion was feared. The policy of repression, abandoned after the Pentland Rising, was renewed with an ever-greater sense of urgency. A shooting incident at Kinloch in October 1677 helped to increase the political temperature, raised still further by alarmist reports sent in by the Earl of Nithsdale and others on conditions in the west, as the Duke of Hamilton reported.

Ther wes a great allarum att Edinburgh that the West was about rising in arms. The bishops bleu the coill, and Earl Nithsdale wes chief informer, for he sed ther wer conventicles keapt consisting of over 3000, wherof 1000 wes weall mounted and armed as any in the nation to his certain knowledge. Some others told that some gentlemens houses were provided with arms far abov the condition of pryvett families; that in some wer 20 carbyns besyd mussequetts and fyrelocks. Bott the principall point

wes moir considerable, which is that with this year or
thereby 7000 horses ar transported from Ireland; hitherto
non can gett account of them bott that they ar in the
hands of disaffected persons in the western and southern
shyrs.[1]

Becoming increasingly bad tempered and eccentric with
age, Lauderdale decided on more desperate measures.
Towards the end of 1677 he wrote to a number of
Highland noblemen, instructing them to assemble their
vassals. In early 1678, these men, supplemented by
regular troops and militia, were sent to south-west
Scotland to be billeted on the recalcitrant communities
of Ayrshire and Lanarkshire. The so-called Highland
Host caused much terror but little real harm, and was
soon withdrawn, but it seemed to indicate just how
impotent the government was. The appearance of the
men from the north, although drawn, in the main, from
the communities of the central Highlands, rather than
the wilder western clans, confirmed every Lowland preju-
dice. William Cleland, a seventeen-year-old student at
St Andrews University, wrote his own satire:

> More savage far those were,
> who with Kolkittoch and Montrose were,
> And sixtie times worse than they
> Whom Turner led in Galloway.
> They durk our Tennants, shame our Wives,
> And were in hazard of our lives,
> They plunder horse, and them they loaden
> With Coverings, Blankets, Sheets and Pladin'
> With Hooding gray, and worsted stuff,
> They sell our Tongs for locks of snuff.
> They take our Cultors and our soaks,
> And from our door they pull the locks,

They leave us neither shoals nor spaids,
And takes away our iron in laids,
They break our pleughs, ev'n when they're working,
We dare not hinder them for durking.[2]

There is no evidence to support Gilbert Burnet's suggestion that Argyll opposed the Highland Host; he was far too dependent on Lauderdale's support for his war on the Macleans. Besides, the relations between the two, which had cooled for a time after Argyll's second marriage, grew warmer in the course of 1678: in March, Archibald Lord Lorne, Argyll's eldest son, married Elizabeth Tollemache, Lauderdale's stepdaughter. This was followed in July by the marriage of one of Argyll's daughters to Lauderdale's nephew, the future fourth earl. Clearly feeling more secure than ever, Argyll pushed for the complete dispossession of the Macleans, using the cover of the Lowland emergency to raise yet more troops.[3] Any reservations his fellow peers might have had about this were soon pushed to the side by the dramatic events unfolding in England.

By the summer of 1678 the mood of optimism and goodwill towards the Stewarts, so obvious at the Restoration, had largely disappeared. Feeling against Catholics was a constant, although largely dormant, feature of English political life. This began to change in the 1670s as reports began to circulate about Catholic influence at court. By far the most serious of these was the persistent rumour that James, Duke of York, the king's brother, had secretly converted to the Church of Rome. As Charles' only living brother this was bad enough, but it became positively explosive when it became increasingly evident that the king was unlikely ever to produce a legitimate heir.

In these more tolerant times it is difficult to understand the intense hostility with which Catholicism was viewed in seventeenth-century Protestant Britain. It wasn't simply a question of faith: Catholicism was perceived to be a political and ideological threat to a whole way of life. James' conversion was to have a profound impact on contemporary opinion, formed, among other things, by Foxe's *Book of Martyrs*, with its lurid depiction of the crimes of Bloody Mary, England's last Catholic sovereign. Above all, for those jealous of English liberties, popery was the cradle of all the worst features of contemporary European politics, as Sir Henry Capel made clear in the House of Commons debate of 27 April 1679: 'From popery came the notion of a standing army and arbitrary power . . . Formerly the crown of Spain, and now France, supports this root of popery among us; but lay popery flat, and there's an end of arbitrary government and power. It is a mere chimera or notion without popery.'[4]

Gripped by a mood of anxiety, in early 1673 the English parliament not only rejected Charles' recent Declaration of Indulgence, which allowed a limited measure of toleration to Catholics and English Protestant dissenters, but went on to pass a Test Act. This required all office holders to take an oath of allegiance repudiating the Pope and Catholic doctrine, and imposed an obligation to take the sacrament in the Church of England. What followed was an earthquake, whose shocks and aftershocks were to shake the English political landscape for the next ten years. That Easter John Evelyn, the diarist, went to the Chapel Royal with one purpose in mind:

> [to] see whither (according to custome) the Duke of Yorke did receive the Communion, with the King, but he did not, to the amazement of everybody; this being the second

year he had foreborn and putt it off, and this being within a day of the Parliament's sitting, who had lately made so severe an Act against the increase of Poperie, gave exceeding griefe and scandal to the whole Nation; that the heyre of it . . . should apostatise; What the consequences of this will be God only knows and wise men dread.[5]

That June, James resigned his post of Lord High Admiral because he would not take the Test. At once there was an almost complete reversal in the whole political climate. Since 1672 England had been allied with France in a war with Holland. The struggle with the Dutch, a leading commercial rival, had been reasonably popular hitherto. Now it took on an entirely different complexion. For many the economic differences were secondary to the consideration that England was fighting with Catholic France against a Protestant neighbour. Catholicism, so long on the fringes, moved steadily to the centre of English political life. Feeling against James, already strong in many quarters, became positively hysterical in 1678, when an unwholesome individual by the name of Titus Oates revealed details of what became known as the Popish Plot. Among other things it was alleged that there was a widespread Catholic conspiracy to murder Charles and replace him with James. This elaborate fabric of lies soon took hold of the nation, and the terror that followed claimed a number of innocent victims, both great and small. Mary of Modena, York's wife, captured the mood of the times in a letter to her brother:

There are so many intrigues, bogus plots and accusations, that I cannot describe a hundredth part of them . . . Things are getting worse . . . Each day they unveil new plots . . . all the posts are closed and all letters opened, so one dares not write anything. You can imagine how anxious I am for the Duke – he has so many enemies . . . I grieve for the extreme suffering of the poor Catholics; they are all banished from London and may not come within ten miles. Many are dying of hunger and privation . . . I close, unable to write of other things, and not daring to say more about this.[6]

Before long a movement took shape to exclude James altogether from the succession. It was headed by Anthony Ashley Cooper, the first Earl of Shaftesbury, an irascible and intolerant man, but one of the most brilliant parliamentarians in English political history. In place of the Catholic York, Shaftesbury and his friends eventually put forward James Scott, Duke of Monmouth and Buccleuch, Charles' bastard – but Protestant – son.

Monmouth was the oldest and the favourite of the king's many illegitimate children; although not entirely without charm or ability, his character had been ruined by the excessive adulation he had received at his father's court. He was vain and superficial; above all, he lacked the determination and drive necessary to turn ordinary men into great ones. Charles James Fox wrote of him: 'Appearing at Court in the bloom of youth, with a beautiful figure, and engaging manners, known to be the darling of the monarch, it is no wonder that he was early assailed by the arts of flattery; and it is rather a proof that he had not the strongest of all minds, or that of any extraordinary weakness of character that he was not proof against them.'[7]

Monmouth believed, or was led to believe, that his mother Lucy Walter – who had died some years before – had secretly married the king in his youth. At the height of the Popish Plot, Charles, strongly committed to the

43

legitimate succession, denied on oath that such a marriage had ever taken place. This made absolutely no difference to Monmouth, captivated by minds far stronger than his own. For Shaftesbury and his friends he was never more than a convenient hook on which to hang their ambitions. In time to come Argyll, taking the place of Shaftesbury, was to be the author of the final, most tragic chapter of Monmouth's life.

Although there was no Scottish equivalent of the Popish Plot, events in London had a direct bearing on Argyll's struggle with the Macleans and their Highland allies. What many in Scotland had come to see as personal ambition was rapidly transformed into public duty, for the Macleans and Macdonalds were all Catholic, or so it was believed. In the spring of 1679, Argyll received a commission to apprehend Lord Macdonnell, Macdonald of Keppoch as well as several Maclean chiefs, and was formally congratulated by the king for his role in pacifying the Highlands.[8] But the combination against him was still too strong, and there were points when his own heartlands were in danger of destruction, much as they had been in the time of Montrose and Alasdair MacColla. To avert this he appealed for the aid of government troops. This request came at the worst possible time, for the tinder-dry Lowlands were erupting in flames.

Lauderdale's Highland Host had underlined the incapacity of the authorities to find an effective solution to religious dissent. In the months that followed the general mood of the Covenanter underground was becoming ever more threatening. In one particularly notorious case a group of twenty armed men attacked Major Johnston, one of the officers in the Edinburgh city guard, threatening to kill him if he took any further action against conventicles. Brave enough to refuse, he was badly wounded. The most serious incident to date came at Lesmahagow in Clydesdale on 30 March 1679. A party of dragoons under one Lieutenant Dalzell heard that a conventicle was due to be held in the area, and rode off, hoping to intercept the rebels. When they arrived they found a small army rather than disorganised men, women and children. The Whigs had organised themselves with military precision, with three companies of foot as well as a troop of horse, far stronger than Dalzell's small force. Hoping to cut off stragglers, Dalzell remained on the margins of the assembly, but his presence was soon discovered and he was quickly surrounded. Hopelessly outnumbered, Dalzell bravely called on the Covenanters to disperse in the name of the king, 'whereupon the commander of the Whiggs horse ansured disdainfully, Farts in the king's teeth, and the Counsells, and all that hes sent you, for wee appear here for the King of Heaven.'[9] In the brief scuffle that followed, Dalzell was wounded and seven of his men taken prisoner, while the rest made off as best they could. One of the commanders of the rebel foot was the same William Cleland who had parodied the Highland Host.

Other incidents followed, increasingly serious in nature. In early May, Archbishop James Sharp, much hated as a Judas by the rebels, was dragged from his coach and murdered on his way back to St Andrews, a particularly brutal episode. Hard on this, a party of dragoons, led by John Graham of Claverhouse, one of the officers assigned to police the south-west, was badly cut up on 1 June by armed Covenanters at Drumclog in Ayrshire. These two incidents sparked the greatest Whig rebellion of the Restoration, when several thousand armed men advanced on Glasgow and took control of virtually the whole of south-west Scotland.

Argyll, wrapped up in his own affairs, was apparently indifferent to the national crisis, or so it seemed to his fellow peers. He was ordered by the Privy Council to break off all operations against the Macleans and Macdonalds, and join the Earl of Linlithgow, the commander-in-chief in Scotland, in the Lowlands with all the forces he could raise. As if anticipating some reluctance on Argyll's part, the orders continued: 'We doubt not of your lordship's readiness, upon all occasions to give commendable proofs of your loyalty and duty to his sacred majesty, and you cannot give a more signal testimony thereof, and of your zeal for the peace and happiness of this kingdom, than by a seasonable assistance against these rebels, and so we cannot but expect a cheerful and ready compliance from your lordship with so just and necessary desire.'[10]

Sensing an opportunity, Lord Macdonnell and the Macleans wrote to the Council, saying that they were only resisting Argyll to avoid being 'forever ruined and enslaved to him', and offered to serve in arms against the rebellious Whigs if the Campbell chief simply remained inactive, 'which he hath ever done when his majesty had any thing to do'. Some of the Privy Council looked with favour on this proposal, no doubt those most suspicious of Argyll; but in the end it was simply too much for most to see men recently condemned as 'papist rebels' advancing into the Lowlands.[11] In the end, even Argyll's assistance was not required; for the rebellion was defeated before it had a chance to take hold.

To deal with the emergency, Charles sent Monmouth to Scotland to take charge of the army. From Stirling, he advanced westwards to meet the rebels, camped at Bothwell near the banks of the River Clyde. Rather than build on their early successes by preparing for the inevitable counter stroke, the Whigs spent the whole time engaging in religious debate, like some mad General Assembly. The inevitable followed; on 22 June Monmouth defeated them with some ease at the Battle of Bothwell Brig. The victorious duke, always mindful of his popularity, behaved with some lenience towards the defeated rebels, and, before leaving Scotland, was instrumental in the introduction of a third Indulgence, which permitted house conventicles under certain conditions. On his return to London he was widely acclaimed by the people, who lit bonfires for the 'Protestant Duke' and toasted him as 'Prince of Wales.' Charles had, in the meantime, exiled the 'Catholic Duke' to the Low Countries to try to take some of the heat out of the ongoing exclusion crisis.

After the Battle of Bothwell Brig Argyll had a free hand to deal with his Highland enemies. The war with the Macleans, which had pursued its intermittent course for some five years, was now close to a climax. Mull was invaded and overrun. In July, Maclean of Ardgour surrendered Kinlochaline Castle in Ardnamurchan before Lord Macdonnell could arrive to relieve him. Only Cairnburgh Castle managed to hold out against the Campbells; but the war was effectively over. Still, Argyll, who had apparently made no preparations to join Linlithgow, was now in a very weak position politically, having placed his own interests first. This would not be forgotten. It was especially dangerous as Lauderdale's remarkable career was now close to its end. In his place came James, Duke of York.

For Argyll the political climate was changing with bewildering rapidity. No sooner was his position improved by the revelations of the Popish Plot than it was undermined by the Covenanters, more openly

treasonable than even the most committed Scottish
Catholic. Opposition to his conduct and policies was now
voiced in the Privy Council, where some suggested that
his official commission should be withdrawn. Moreover,
he was far too closely associated with Lauderdale to hope
for any encouragement or support from Shaftesbury and
his allies. In the House of Lords, Shaftesbury had
launched a powerful attack on the old Secretary and the
perceived misgovernment in Scotland. Popery, he argued,
was to precede slavery in England, whereas slavery was
the forerunner of popery in Scotland. Having so clearly
lost control in the north, Lauderdale was soon to fade
from the scene. Argyll was now standing on dangerously
narrow ground.

Even before Monmouth left for Scotland his father
had been worried by his political associations, which at
times led him to side with Shaftesbury in openly opposing
royal policy in Privy Council debates. Bothwell Brig,
while satisfying, was only likely to increase the power of
Shaftesbury and the opposition; so before Monmouth
returned to London in triumph, Charles dissolved parliament, bringing the first phase of the exclusion crisis to
an end. Some of the king's leading ministers, most
notably George Saville, Marquis of Halifax, while suspicious of James, were fearful that Shaftesbury would
seize any opportunity to make Monmouth king, as a
puppet for his own party. Later that summer, when
Charles suddenly took ill, Halifax and his colleagues
summoned James back from the continent. The king
recovered, and as London was still too dangerous for
James to remain, he was sent away again. This time,
though, he was sent to Scotland with a definite role to
perform; unlike Monmouth, who, for his conduct in the
city, was banished to Holland.

Although there is little doubt he would have preferred to remain in London, James was to make good use of his time in Scotland. While feeling against Catholics was no less strong in Scotland as it was in England, the general political climate was quite different. Parliament was still very much a feudal body, with little of the independent spirit of its English counterpart. Much of the nobility, economically impoverished, depended on court patronage. Above all, Lauderdale, in his years as Secretary of State and High Commissioner, had made Scotland generally more receptive to royal absolutism than England ever could be. James, soon to succeed the ailing Lauderdale as High Commissioner, set about building on this legacy, determined to ensure that if it ever came to a violent contest over the succession, Scotland would be firmly in his camp. Much depended on cultivating all of the loyal forces, including the beleaguered Macleans.

As soon as James arrived it looked as if he and Argyll were on a collision course. The matter concerned the duke's right to sit on the Scottish Privy Council without first taking the oath of allegiance, which, among other things, contained a denunciation of popery. Argyll took exception to James' refusal to take the oath, and, supported by Sir George Mackenzie, the Lord Advocate, even raised the matter with Lauderdale.[12] It seems odd that Argyll should have chosen to make a stand on this issue, while others, no less committed to Protestantism, simply chose to ignore it. He must surely have been aware that James' appearance in Scotland would inevitably push Lauderdale into the background, and it was therefore not wise to attack such a powerful figure. He probably assumed that James had been weakened politically by the Popish Plot; if so, it was a serious error of judgement – the first of several. Scotland, as James was soon to show, was not England, and Argyll was not Shaftesbury.

James, who had refused the Test Act in England, did not feel himself bound to take any oath denouncing his faith, taking his seat regardless of the objections raised. Despite this, he appears to have borne Argyll no ill will, writing: 'I find him a man of very good parts, and willing and able to serve his majesty.'[13] James, a man without a great deal of imagination or intellectual subtlety, tended to take a rather straightforward view of affairs, and clearly saw Argyll as a pillar of the royal establishment in Scotland. There is absolutely nothing in the evidence to suggest that he viewed Argyll as a dangerous political opponent, like Shaftesbury in England. On the contrary, Argyll's power was good: it was just that he had too much of it. He was to be curbed, not destroyed. For Argyll's opponents and creditors, however, so long frustrated by the obduracy of Lauderdale, this changing emphasis came as an ideal opportunity. In setting about reducing the accumulated Campbell power, James started to play a game, the rules of which were determined by others less well intentioned towards the house of Argyll.

By February 1680, James had already worked out the outlines of a new Highland policy, intended to reverse the neglect of Lauderdale. He wrote to Charles, urging him to depend on 'loyal families'. Most important of all:

> The extraordinary favours and partialities formerly shewn to my Lord Argile, could neither be answer'd nor without much difficulty amended, since that family had been so much advanced and so much power put imprudently into their hands.[14]

James was thus suggesting a complete reversal of the policy hitherto pursued by Lauderdale. He went on to say that Charles should pay what was due to Argyll, and thus save the ancient and loyal Clan Maclean. Their gratitude would thus be secured. More important, if 'the Earle of Argile haue the MacLanes estate, he would be greater than it were fit for a subject to be'. A compromise was reached, and Argyll, sensitive to the change in the climate, stopped short of the outright destruction of Clan Gillean. Sir John Maclean was granted an estate on Tiree, financed by both Argyll and the king. This in itself was no longer enough; James left Scotland in early 1680: when he returned the real attack on Argyll was to begin.

4

The fall of Argyll

During his first brief stay in Scotland James had done very well, acting with tact and moderation, in refreshing contrast to the bad-tempered and tyrannical Lauderdale. Bit by bit he created his own party, introducing into government men who had been frozen out by the Secretary. Among others this included John Murray, Marquis of Atholl, a long-standing rival of Argyll's, with whom he had come close to fighting a duel. Lauderdale, moreover, ailing in mind and body, was gradually fading from the scene. In September 1680 he resigned the post of Secretary of State for Scotland, removing a great safety net that Argyll had found so useful on more than one occasion. James' expressed concern for the future of the Macleans provided a sure indication that the old Secretary's Highland policy was soon to be abandoned.

Argyll should have been attentive to the change in the political climate, and the possible dangers to his own position but as a politician Argyll's talents were at best limited. Above all, he had the worst possible vice for a man in his position – an overwhelming conviction that he was always in the right. It was this, perhaps as much as the scheming of his enemies, which was to bring him, for the second time in his life, to the threshold of destruction.

In England the Popish Plot had not yet gone off the boil, and Shaftesbury continued to push for exclusion. New stories were circulating of a mysterious 'black box', which many talked about but none had seen. This allegedly contained details of Charles' marriage to Lucy Walter, thus proving Monmouth's legitimacy. Charles dismissed it as a farce, and published a denial that any such marriage had taken place. More than this, in a clear mood of anger, he instructed the Earl of Macclesfield, who had been one of his counsellors during his exile, and had known Lucy Walter, to let it be known that she had been little better than a whore.[1] Macclesfield refused to perform this dishonourable service. Charles was further angered after Monmouth, who had returned from exile unbidden, set out on a tour of the west country, drumming up support for his cause in a seventeenth-century version of a whistle-stop tour. Things were no better when parliament reassembled in October 1680, and once again turned its sights on James, defying the king's instructions not to interfere with the succession. Those who followed Shaftesbury in pressing the king to accept exclusion, loosely known as the 'country party', were now given a new name by their opponents – the Whigs, after the extreme Covenanters. Insult was traded for insult. Soon the supporters of Charles and the legitimate succession were being called Tories, after a group of Irish bandits. Both labels stuck.

With the political temperature in London close to boiling, Charles decided that it was best to send James back to Scotland. To emphasise that he was not in disgrace he was appointed High Commissioner in place of Lauderdale. James arrived in October, accompanied by his wife Mary of Modena, no doubt relieved to escape the tension at court. This time he was to spend far longer in the ancient realm of the Stewarts, setting about deepening the base of support he had established during his first visit. He continued to behave with discretion and charm, and some of the stories later recorded by Gilbert Burnet and Robert Wodrow to his discredit are almost certainly fabrications. As the months passed, however, people had a better chance to judge his character, and what they saw was not entirely to his good. In some ways he resembled Argyll, with the same obstinacy and simple-minded conviction in the justice of his own cause. In other ways he was just the opposite: while Argyll was generally unwilling to heed advice, James was all too ready to be moulded by others, especially when he was convinced they were acting in his interests. At the parliament of 1681, it was recorded of him: 'Some wise men observed, that the Duke of York might have honestie, justice, and courage enough, and his Father's preptorinesse, but that he had nather great conduct, nor deep reach in affairs, but was a silly [simple] man.'[2]

For Argyll's enemies and creditors, a new opportunity had come. James' well-known concern for the welfare of the Macleans was soon to be extended into a more general attack on the Campbell chief. In early 1681, the Duchess of Lauderdale was even moved to write to an unnamed correspondent: 'I wish the Earl of Argyll would sell his estates, so as his family may not be prey to his enemies, who are too many, and may be too powerful, if he take not good and speedy heed.'[3]

The story that James promised to make Argyll 'the greatest man in Scotland' if he turned Catholic is clearly a later invention.[4] James was always eager to defend his fellow Catholics, and welcomed converts, without bothering overmuch about their motives; for him to attempt to convert a man like Argyll at this time would, however, have been politically suicidal. Moreover, it clearly flew in the face of his declared policy, which was to reduce and not increase the power of the Campbells. All the evidence suggests that he looked on Argyll with some favour, regardless of their confessional differences, at least until after the opening of the 1681 parliament.[5]

When parliament assembled all the latent hostility towards Argyll, suppressed by Lauderdale in the parliament of 1669, came to the surface. He faced several attacks, one following hard upon the heels of another. Previously Lauderdale would most likely have overruled such attempts, but James acted more like a neutral referee. Argyll's creditors, headed by the Earl of Errol, placed a demand for unpaid debts before the Lords of the Articles, the body responsible for managing the parliamentary agenda, although this was subsequently dismissed on investigation. More seriously, Sir George Mackenzie, the Lord Advocate, received instructions to deprive the earl of the hereditary office of Sheriff and Justice General of Argyllshire and the Isles, which had been in his family for centuries. This too was dropped. It was then alleged that part of the former Marquis of Argyll's estate had been annexed to the crown, and was thus improperly restored to his son. When the act of forfeiture was examined it was found that the lands in question had been left at the king's disposal. In anger, and in truth, Argyll responded that annexation of these lands to the crown was the last thing his father's enemies would have desired, as they clearly wanted the spoil for themselves.[6] Finally, it was proposed that an inquiry be set up into the manner in which the earl was exercising his heritable jurisdictions. But James, who had initially approved this, just as quickly changed his mind, and the proposal was suppressed when it went before parliament. All this should have shown Argyll how vulnerable his position really was. If James' conduct was indeed an attempt to alert the earl to the fact that he depended on the royal favour, it failed in its purpose: soon he and James were on a collision course. The matter concerned the Test Act, one of the most infamous measures in Scottish political history.

It began simply enough. James' purpose in introducing the Test was to bind all public figures in support of royal authority and the legitimate succession. In opposing this measure, Andrew Fletcher of Saltoun proposed that the security of the Protestant religion be made part of the Test. But how was this to be defined? Sir James Dalrymple, Lord President of the Court of Session and a man with a brilliant legal mind, immediately suggested that it should take the form of the 1560 Confession of Faith, ratified by the first parliament of James VI in 1567. Apart from Sir James himself few, if any, of the members present, including the bishops, had ever read this document or were even vaguely aware of its contents. Nevertheless, without pausing for thought, parliament, with the approval of York, immediately adopted it as part of the Test. Dalrymple's amendment had made a mockery of the Test, as he clearly knew it would. For the Confession of Faith admitted no head of the church other than the Lord Jesus, and no form of church government other than Presbyterianism. Worst of all, from James' point of view, it actively encouraged the faithful to resist tyranny. Writing later in the eighteenth century, Sir John Dalrymple, the Lord President's descendant, summarised the matter very well: 'Thus modelled, the Test was a bundle of inconsistencies; for it inferred an obligation, upon those who took it, to conform to any religion the King pleased, and yet adhere to the Presbyterian religion; to oppose prelacy, and yet maintain the present condition of the church, which was prelacy; and to renounce and yet affirm the doctrine of non-resistance.'[7]

Even if James could be expected to know the wording of the Confession of Faith, the historical context in which it was adopted should have alerted his suspicions. It was formulated at a time when many of the Scots nobility were in revolt against the government of the Catholic Mary of Guise, the then queen regent, and ratified by parliament shortly after the forced abdication of her daughter, Mary Queen of Scots.

When the nature of Dalrymple's time bomb became known, there were many who simply refused to take the Test, including the Duke of Hamilton. During the debate in parliament, Argyll had suggested that each king's sons and brothers should be made to take the Test, thus adhering to Protestantism, although he was prepared to make an exception for James himself. This amendment was defeated; but it probably marks the point when the duke began to perceive Argyll as a potential enemy to the Catholic succession. Before long, he was subject to extraordinary proceedings. Argyll, as a privy councillor and a commissioner of the Treasury, was pressed to take the Test at an early stage, although he was not legally bound to do so until 1 January 1682. Before this, shortly after parliament was dissolved, he was dismissed, along with Sir James Dalrymple, from the Court of Session, where he had occupied the position of an extraordinary lord since 1674. In addition, the Privy Council was summoned at short notice to hear Argyll take the Test.

He at once sought a meeting with James, asking why he was being subjected to such pressure, especially as there were matters in it which the High Commissioner himself disliked, to which he replied in anger 'Most true; that Test was brought into the Parliament without the Confession of Faith; but the late President caused put in the Confession, which makes it such that no honest man can take it.'[8]

Even so, Argyll found himself with little choice. When he appeared before the Council on 3 November, the Bishop of Edinburgh, who had discussed the matter with James, assured him that he could take the Test subject to an explanation. Before kneeling to take the Test, Argyll made the following declaration:

> I am confident the Parliament never intended to impose contradictory oathes, and therefore I think no body can explain it bot for himselfe and reconcile it as it is genuine and agrees in its own sense. I take it insofar as it is consistent with itselfe and the Protestant religion, and I doe declare that I mean not to bind up myselfe in my station and in a lawful way to wish to endeavour any alteration I think to the advantage of church or state not repugnant to the Protestant religion and my loyaltie, and this I understand as part of my oath.[9]

James appeared to accept this qualification with a good grace, admitting Argyll to his place on the Privy Council. Argyll relaxed, clearly believing himself safe; but he had, in effect, handed his enemies a loaded gun. This was the moment they had waited for. James was apparently persuaded that Argyll's words had been treasonable. When the Council assembled the following day there was an ominous change of mood. When Argyll took the Test for a second time, in his capacity as a commissioner of the Treasury, he was asked to repeat the explanation he had made the day before. Argyll, clearly aware that something was wrong, initially refused, until ordered to do so by James, on the grounds that some present had not been able to hear him. He duly complied, but when asked to sign the document he refused until such time as he had consulted with his lawyers. Having failed to give satisfaction according to the Act of Parliament, Argyll was at once dismissed from both the Privy Council and the Treasury.

In theory exclusion from public office is the only penalty that Argyll should have suffered. Many of his fellow peers refused to take the Test altogether, and others in public life took it subject to some explanation, without suffering any loss of position or prestige. But Argyll's enemies, not content with his removal from office, pushed the matter further. Sir George Mackenzie of Tarbat, a one-time ally of the Earl of Middleton and a long-standing opponent of the Campbell chief, and Sir George Gordon of Haddo, who had replaced Dalrymple as President of the Court of Session, persuaded James that Argyll's reflections on the Test were not just ill advised but treasonable.[10] A few days later, he was arrested and imprisoned in Edinburgh Castle, for the third time in his life. On the day of his arrest, the Council wrote to Charles, saying that his explanation to the Test was a gross reflection on the Act of Parliament, making it 'contain things contradictory and inconsistent.'[11]

It was clear to all, not least James, that this was perfectly true. Argyll's greatest crime was that he was naïve enough to make a public declaration to this effect, although he must have known that there were all too many ready to use it against him. His best defence would have been to decline the Test without explanation. After all, James had himself refused to swear to the English Test of 1673. But Argyll's conceit and self-importance encompassed his own destruction. History was repeating itself: as he did in 1662, he walked into a trap largely of his own making. The difference now was that he had no powerful friend at court. In London, Lauderdale did his best to help the beleaguered house of Campbell, but he was now a figure with little real influence. Charles agreed that Argyll should be charged with leasing-making, although, as in 1662, he gave instructions that no sentence should be carried out without his express approval.[12]

Argyll's trial opened on 12 December 1681. For James, impatient of the time-wasting formality of Scots Law, the outcome seemed to be a foregone conclusion. Before the verdict was announced he wrote to Lord Dartmouth in England 'Lord Argyle's trial began yesterday and their forms in the justice court are so tedious that they could not make an end of it then, but will, as I believe this evening; and I have reason to believe that the jury will find the bill . . . and that the little Lord will once again be at His Majesty's mercy.'[13]

It was clear to many at the time that the case against him was largely based on malice. As if to emphasise this, the Lord Justice General, who presided over the panel of judges, had himself made an explanation on taking the Test.[14] The prosecution was led by Sir George Mackenzie, the Lord Advocate. There was a special irony in this, for Mackenzie, as a young lawyer, had defended Argyll's father in 1661. His task now was to prove before the judges that the charge was relevant, that Argyll's actions had constituted leasing-making. The judges were evenly divided on the question, and the Justice General, seemingly too embarrassed to exercise his casting vote, summoned Lord Nairn, something of a legal fossil, who had neither the stamina nor the patience to sit through the whole proceedings. He was brought to the court in the middle of the night, and kept falling asleep as the clerk read out the summaries of his fellow judges. On being wakened he duly voted for condemnation, presumably anxious to get back to bed. Once this was out of the way what followed was a mere technicality; the jury declared Argyll guilty of treason and leasing-making. The Privy Council then wrote to the king, advising him of the outcome, and asked him to give orders for sentence of death and forfeiture to be pronounced.

News of the verdict soon spread throughout the United Kingdom. In London, Lord Halifax told the king that while he did not understand Scots law, he knew that the laws of England would not have hanged a dog for such a crime.[15] Gilbert Burnet, no friend of James, said that the sentence was universally condemned and many spoke of the duke with horror.[16] Sir John Lauder of Fountainhall made his own observations on the matter: 'This is a strange reverse of providence: Argyle, a great courtier in July last, and carries the crown before the Duke before the Riding of the Parliament, and now condemned of treason and forfaulted, and overrun by the violent malice of his enemies.'[17]

Interestingly, Shaftesbury and the Whigs seem not to have been unduly concerned, clearly seeing Argyll as just another discredited ally of Lauderdale. Charles and James, it was later claimed, had no intention of allowing the full sentence to be carried out, simply intending to use this opportunity to deprive Argyll of some of his extensive powers.[18] This may be so; but matters had changed since this was first proposed in 1680. Argyll was now more than an over-mighty subject: he was a perceived enemy of the Catholic succession. In England, a recent attempt to prosecute Shaftesbury for treason had failed, so James may have been all the more keen to ensure that there would be no way out for Argyll. It is certainly true that his enemies, anxious to ensure that this second downfall of the Campbells would not be followed by a second restoration, continued to pour poison into the duke's ear. We cannot be absolutely certain, therefore, what would really have happened if Argyll had remained in royal custody. Believing himself to be in peril of his life he was 'persuaded' to escape, thus ensuring his condemnation as a fugitive from royal justice.

What follows gives all the appearance of a well-laid scheme. More troops began to arrive in Edinburgh, while rooms were being prepared in the Tolbooth, the common jail, where peers were traditionally sent just prior to their executions. An unnamed informant carried news of these preparations to Argyll himself: 'And a person of quality, whom lord Argyle never named, affirmed to him, on his honour, that he had heard one, who was in great favour, say to the duke, the thing must be done, and that it would be easier to satisfy the king about it after it was done, than to obtain his leave for doing it. It is certain, many of the Scottish nobility believe that it was intended he should die.'[19]

Fearful for his life, the earl's friends added to his anxieties by urging him to escape. Horses and guides were prepared to take him south across the border and on to London. Argyll at first seemed uncertain about this, but finally agreed. On Tuesday 20 December he sent word to Lady Sophia Lindsay, his favourite step-daughter, to come to the castle accompanied by a page. When they were alone in the cell, Argyll changed clothes with the page, making his way out in this comic opera fashion. It all seems a little too easy; the page with whom he changed places was as tall as Argyll was short, so even the most superficial observer would presumably have been able to spot the difference.[20] It was later suggested that Lady Sophia be publicly whipped for her part in the affair, a proposal James himself resisted; but no punishment appears to have been meted out to the castle guards for allowing so distinguished a prisoner to escape in so simple a fashion.

Argyll made his way out of Edinburgh in the dark, to begin his long ride to London, aided on his way by Covenanter preachers and old Cromwellian officers. He had become what he had never intended to be – a Protestant martyr. The day after his escape, the king's letter arrived in Edinburgh, authorising a sentence of death and forfeiture, instructing that this should be delayed until further notice. But with Argyll on the run, his enemies now had all they wanted. On Thursday 23 December the sentence was proclaimed at the Market Cross. The road back was now closed; Campbell power was gone, perhaps forever.

This second fall of the house of Argyll was a source of both anger and amusement, especially at the obvious injustice entailed. One John Philip, a former minister, was ill-advised enough to declare openly that 'the Duke of Albany [York's Scottish title] was a bloody and cruell man and a great tyrant and was distasteful to the subjects . . . and also that the Earle of Argyle was unjustly forfaulted and that there was no law for forfaulting him'.[21] These indiscreet remarks carried savage consequences: Philip was fined £2000 sterling, a truly prodigious sum for the times, and ordered to be imprisoned on the Bass Rock for life. In Edinburgh the boys of Heriot's Hospital decided that the school watchdog had a position of public trust and should therefore be made to take the Test. As the animal maintained a stony silence when the matter was put to it, this was taken as a flat refusal. However, its advocate, clearly skilled in the law, argued that this silence might be taken as assent as much as refusal. The Test was then smeared in butter, which was described as Argyll's explanation, and presented once more. As soon as the butter was licked off the animal spat out the Test, and was duly condemned to be 'hanged like a dog' for leasing-making. In recording this incident, Sir John Lauder says that sentence was carried out. Happy to say, the poor beast, like Argyll, made good his escape, although his office, all his assets, both heritable and moveable, and all his feudal privileges were declared to be forfeit.[22] The parallel was taken still further when £500 was offered for the recapture of 'ane cutt lugged, brounish coloured Mastiff Tyke, called Watch, short leged, and of low stature . . .' ; £500 being the same sum that was now being offered for the apprehension of Argyll.

In general, however, the fall of Argyll passed off without too much concern, and seems to have been largely unnoticed by the Covenanter underground, too pre-occupied with its own problems. In the Highlands those who might have been expected to benefit from the lifting of the Campbell yoke were soon disappointed. Many of his former superiorities simply passed to other magnates, and the Catholic Duke of Gordon was soon lording over Lochaber in no better manner than Argyll.

While the old power structure was collapsing in the Highlands, William Veitch, a dissident Presbyterian preacher, guided the fugitive earl on his way to London, making good use of his many contacts, both in England and Scotland. For his safety, Argyll adopted a disguise, but appears to have been recognised on more than one occasion, though luckily for him only by sympathisers.

Once in London he was safe; at least, for the time being. However, the political climate in England had undergone a profound change since James had come to Scotland, with important consequences for the future of both Argyll and Monmouth.

5

Conspiracy and exile

The period immediately after James' second departure for Scotland marks the high noon of the Popish Plot. London, in particular, was a stronghold of exclusionist activity. At the King's Head tavern, Shaftesbury and his supporters, like the Jacobins of a future age, had regular social and political gatherings of what they called the Green Ribbon Club. There were grandees, like Lord William Russell and Ford, Lord Grey of Tankerville and Arthur Capel, Earl of Essex, as well as gentry of the middle rank, most notably Sir Thomas Armstrong, a friend of Monmouth's. There was also a scattering of old Cromwellian officers, supporters of what was called the Good Old Cause, including Colonel Algernon Sidney, who, like King Charles, had once been a lover of Lucy Walter; Colonel Richard Rumbold, who all those years before had faced Lord Lorne across the battle lines at Dunbar. Rumbold went on to fight at Worcester, and was on duty that cold January day when Charles I was led to his death. Other veterans of the New Model army joined him: Colonel John Rumsey, Colonel Venner, Major John Wildman and Captain John Jones. For these men, Monmouth was simply a convenient front, masking their republican sympathies. From time to time, the Club was graced by the presence of the loathsome Titus Oates, possibly the most repulsive cleric in history, whose holy orders had once allowed him to escape hanging for sodomy, a capital crime in the seventeenth century. John Dryden, the poet, was later to write a brilliant satire of these men and their schemes, based upon the biblical story of Absalom and Achitopel. A few lines capture the spirit of the Whigs and the Popish Plot.

> The Jews, a headstrong, moody, murmuring race
> As ever tried th' extent and stretch of grace,
> God's pampered people, whom, debauched with ease,
> No King could govern nor no God could please . . .
> Began to dream they wanted liberty . . .
> The Good old Cause revived, a Plot requires.
> Plots, true or false, are necessary things
> To raise up Commonwealths and ruin Kings . . .
> From hence began that Plot, the Nation's curse,
> Bad in itself but repeated worse
> Raised in extremes, and in extremes, decried,
> With Oaths affirmed, with dying vows denied.
> Not weighed or winnowed by the multitude;
> But swallowed in the mass, unchewed and crude.
> Some truth there was, but dashed and brewed with lies;
> To please the fools and puzzle all the wise . . .
> This Plot which failed, for want of common sense
> Had yet a deep and dangerous consequence . . .
> Some by their friends, more by themselves thought wise,
> Opposed the Power to which they could not rise.[1]

There were also a number of Scots dissidents who

associated themselves with the Whigs. The most promi-
nent of these was Patrick Hume, the eldest son of Sir
Patrick Hume of Polwarth in Berwickshire. He had been
elected as Member of Parliament for Berwickshire in
1665, and was active in opposing the extreme measures
taken by the government against the Covenanters. His
continuing opposition eventually led to periods of
imprisonment in Stirling, Edinburgh and Dumbarton.
Eventually released in the summer of 1679, he left for
London, where he was befriended by Shaftesbury,
Monmouth and Lord Russell.

By far the most curious of the exiles was one Robert
Ferguson, the son of an Aberdeenshire clergyman.
Himself a cleric, he was so noted for his endless cloak-
and-dagger schemes that he is known to history as
Ferguson the Plotter. His singular appearance was later
described when he was being hunted for his life: 'A tall
Lean man, with dark brown hair, a great Roman nose,
thin jawed, heat in his face, speaks in the Scots tone, a
sharp piercing eye, stoops a little in the shoulders, he
hath a shuffling gait, that differs from all men; wears his
periwig down almost over his eyes; about 45 or 46 years
old.'[2]

An endless writer of tracts, Ferguson's first political
pamphlet appeared in the late spring of 1680, entitled *A
Letter to a Person of Honour concerning the Black Box*. He
argued that the black box was a fiction invented by those
out to discredit Monmouth's right to the crown, and to
divert attention from the treasonable practices of the
Duke of York.[3] Soon after this broadside was launched,
Charles again denied that he had ever married Lucy
Walter 'on the faith of a Christian and the word of a
King'. Ferguson responded with *A Letter to a Person of
Honour concerning the King's disavowing his having been*

married to the Duke of Monmouth's Mother. In this he took the argument one step further, hinting that evidence would be forthcoming proving that the marriage had taken place. Needless to say, like the black box itself, no such evidence ever appeared.

For Lord Macaulay, the nineteenth-century Whig historian, Ferguson, although never a figure of the front rank, is almost as big a villain as Titus Oates, and the architect of the conspiracy that eventually drove Monmouth to his ruin.

> He was violent, malignant, regardless of truth, insensible to shame, insatiable of notoriety, delighting in intrigue, in tumult, in mischief for its own sake, he toiled during many years in the darkest mines of faction. He lived among libellers and false witnesses. He was a keeper of a secret purse from which agents too vile to be acknowledged received hire, and the director of a secret press whence pamphlets bearing no name were daily issued.[4]

Dryden, even hotter in his condemnation, compared Ferguson to the greatest traitor of all.

> Shall that false Hebronite escape our curse,
> Judas, that keeps the rebels' pension-purse;
> Judas, that pays the Treason-writer's fee,
> Judas, that well deserves his namesake's Tree.[5]

Shaftesbury, Ferguson and their fellow Whigs had great hopes of the parliament that opened in October 1680. A new Exclusion Bill passed through the Commons with a comfortable majority. It then proceeded to the Lords, for one of the most crucial debates in English history, attended throughout by the king himself. Shaftesbury promoted the Bill with all his formidable rhetorical skills, but Halifax, in opposition, was even greater. Influenced

DVKE OF YORK

James VII & II (as Duke of York), by Sir Peter Lely
(National Galleries of Scotland)

Archibald Campbell, 1st Marquess of Argyll, by David Scougall
(National Galleries of Scotland)

Archibald Campbell, 9th Earl of Argyll, by L. Schuneman
(National Galleries of Scotland)

John Maitland, 1st Duke of Lauderdale, by Sir Peter Lely
(National Galleries of Scotland)

Eilean Dearg (One Tree Island), Loch Riddon, by Hubert Andrew

Old Inveraray, the market-place, 1746. The town bridge can be seen to the right of the Mercat Cross. From a drawing by Paul Sandby.

by the eloquence of Halifax, and the presence of Charles, the Lords rejected exclusion. Soon after, the king dissolved parliament, and summoned a new assembly to meet at Oxford in March 1681. Oxford had been the royalist capital during the Civil War, and was generally more receptive to the Tory cause than Whig London. Charles clearly hoped for a more moderate debate in more moderate surroundings. If so, he was disappointed: the newly elected House of Commons was filled with as many Whigs as its predecessors. A third Exclusion Bill was soon in preparation, but Charles, in a surprise move, averted the crisis by dissolving parliament. No other was summoned for the remainder of the reign, and thus there was no public forum for the opposition to express its dissatisfaction with Stewart rule.

The dissolution of the Oxford parliament arguably marks one of the great anticlimaxes of English history. The great Whig party, which had seemed so formidable, even threatening the country at one point with a new civil war, simply imploded. It had plenty of talent, but its organisation was largely *ad hoc*, depending on the lightning conductor of parliament to channel its energy. The truth is that beyond Shaftesbury and the radicals of the Green Ribbon Club, few in the country ever again desired a return to the anarchy and dictatorship that had emerged out of the Civil War. Moreover, for some time there had been a steady reaction in the country against the excesses of the Popish Plot, especially among the Tory squires, the backbone of civil administration throughout most of the land. Shaftesbury himself was arrested on a charge of high treason, although this was subsequently thrown out by the grand jury in London, still solid in its Whig sympathies. However, with the steady change in the political climate, and the growing strength of the court, the opposition began to move underground, where it steadily lost its grip on reality, becoming ever more desperate in its scheming. It was at this dangerous time that Argyll arrived in London.

Whatever sympathy Argyll might have been expected to receive for his treatment at the hands of James, had now largely evaporated in the heat of the royal reaction. In January 1682, shortly after he came to the capital, it was written:

> My lord Arguile, it's believed, is here; his case is thought very hard, and ye proceedings against him vigorous; and all imputed to the Duke's severity, and so made use of by those that don't love him, as an argument what we might expect from his government here. But Arguile is not much pitted, being looked on generally as a very ill man to ye Crown, and who has made use of the King's favours heretofore to do very greate injustices to others.[6]

Charles himself seems not to have felt himself very much threatened by Argyll's presence. When informed of his whereabouts he is said to have refused to 'hunt a hunted partridge'.[7] It is just as likely, though, that as the attempt to prosecute Shaftesbury had failed, the king had no desire to draw too much attention to the circumstances under which Argyll had been tried and condemned. The earl soon found himself in an odd position. It's almost certain that the circumstances of his arrest and trial had taken him by surprise. He was eventually to appeal to Charles, and may have come to London with the intention of throwing himself on the king's mercy at an early stage. Even in opposing York, he had shown none of the intense hostility towards him so fully demonstrated by Shaftesbury and the Whigs, never at any time suggesting that he should be excluded from the throne. A moderate in his religious views, his apparent conversion to the Protestant cause had come late in life. His relationship with the Whig grandees was never as close as that of his fellow Scot, Patrick Hume of Polwarth. For Argyll, the restoration of his estates and fortunes always came before the wider political cause embraced by the other opponents of the Stewarts. It was only after it became clear that there would never be a resurrection of Campbell power as long as the Stewarts occupied the throne that Argyll began to move steadily in a more radical direction. An outcast, he was forced to depend on William Veitch, who had good contacts in the radical underground. Close to the capital, he was given over to the care of Captain John Lockyer, yet another ex-officer of the New Model Army, and taken to the house of Ann Smith, the wife of a wealthy sugar baker, at Battersea. Argyll and Ann Smith seemed to have formed a close political understanding; it was she, more than any other, who provided him with continual encouragement and support. Most important of all, she was to supply him with the means that allowed him to mount his expedition in 1685.

In general the Whigs seem to have been suspicious of the new arrival. Although a government agent spotted him in April 1682 in the company of Ferguson the Plotter, to begin with – probably more embarrassed than encouraged by some of his new associates – he kept his contacts with the underground to a minimum.[8] Some, like Algernon Sydney, a committed republican, were highly distrustful of an earl, who, whatever his current problems, was conservative and royalist. Even Shaftesbury was inclined to hold him at a distance as the former protégé of Lauderdale. But Argyll was too important an asset to be completely ignored, for he enjoyed a power and status that English noblemen, even the greatest, had lost at the close of the Middle Ages. As Lord Macaulay notes, he had

> an authority which no wealth could give and no attainder could take away, made him, as a leader of an insurrection, truly formidable. No southern lord could feel confident that, if he ventured to resist the government, even his own gamekeeper and huntsmen would stand by him. An Earl of Bedford, an Earl of Devonshire could not engage to bring ten men into the field. MacCallum More, penniless and deprived of his earldom, might, at any moment, raise a serious civil war.[9]

Sometime in the summer of 1682, Argyll and Shaftesbury met to discuss plans for a joint rising in England and Scotland. As early as March, the Campbell chief had begun to consider that it might be necessary to solve his problems in a more militant fashion. On his behalf, arms were purchased in The Netherlands. His agent, John Campbell, a Glasgow merchant, obtained a ship; but nothing further is heard of this scheme after the ship was apparently lost at sea.[10] In meeting Shaftesbury, Argyll said that he would need £30 000 to raise a rebellion in Scotland, although this was reduced by half in the course of their discussions. This meeting seems more in the nature of a mutual exploration, as no serious plans were made. In the end they achieved nothing for the simple reason that the barrier of mutual distrust was simply too great. The two men appear to have avoided each other thereafter.[11]

The other significant meeting Argyll had that summer was with Arthur Forbes, Viscount Granard, an old friend from the days of the Glencairn Rising. Granard was now one of the two Lord Justices of Ireland, and agreed to secure that country in the Protestant interest in the event of a rising in England and Scotland. He also agreed to send over 5000 men to support Argyll.[12] This could have made all the difference to the earl's prospects of success, and it seems that Granard, who had taken trouble to seek Argyll out, was perfectly sincere in his intentions; but he was one of those soon to be implicated in the Rye House Plot. Although never brought to trial, he appears to have been sufficiently intimidated into making a thorough change in his political allegiance. Not only did he bring out troops against Argyll in 1685, but he was also the last Irish Protestant lord to abandon James in 1690.[13]

Throughout the summer of 1682 plots continued to take shape with a feverish intensity, in a largely unco-ordinated fashion. Eager for action, Shaftesbury pushed and prodded the reluctant Monmouth – in the political doghouse, but still his father's beloved son. As always, Ferguson the Plotter was instrumental in communicating between the various participants. The chief scheme entailed a plan by Monmouth, Shaftesbury, Essex, Russell, Sydney, John Hampden and Lord Howard of Escrick to raise the West Country, Cheshire and London. As a preliminary to this, the plotters discussed the possibility of kidnapping the king.

In general, the political aims of those behind these grand schemes were fairly nebulous, resting on little more than a desire to prevent James from succeeding Charles. But beyond Argyll and the Whig grandees there were other, more desperate spirits, whose plans did not stop short of murder. Chief among these was Richard Rumbold, who, from his boldness of spirit and loss of an eye, was known to his friends as Hannibal.[14] Rumbold owned a property near the racecourse at Newmarket known as the Rye House. From here, he and his fellow conspirators, including Colonel John Rumsey, planned to intercept Charles and James – who had now returned from Scotland – and assassinate them on their way back from the races. Rumsey, a grim old republican, suggested that they should finish the job by murdering Monmouth as well, but was persuaded against this by those who wished to hold to the Protestant duke for the present, 'for he cannot endure long'.[15] It is difficult to know if the Rye House Plot would have been pushed to its intended bloody conclusion, or come to nothing, like the other Whig schemes. In the end it was never given a chance; for, following a great fire at Newmarket in March 1683, Charles and James returned to Whitehall before the time intended.

By September 1682, as the Protestant party grew weaker, London was becoming a dangerous place. Charles finally decided the time had come to 'hunt the hunted partridge', and his agents were soon on the trail of Argyll, who, close to discovery, managed to escape to Holland.[16] A few weeks later, Shaftesbury, threatened with a fresh prosecution, followed, dying in exile in January 1683. Sometime after this, almost certainly before the discovery of the Rye House Plot in June, Argyll, clearly tiring of his life as a fugitive, sent an appeal to the king. He requested that the forfeiture against him be reversed as 'my quiet submission doth rather encourage than abate the evil designs of some against me and my family'.[17] But his enemies soon had more than enough evidence against him to ensure that he would remain a permanent exile.

The flight and subsequent death of Shaftesbury deprived the Whigs of his powerful base of support in the capital. Argyll was now more important than ever, and even Algernon Sydney dropped his objections to cooperating with the fugitive earl. In November 1682,

Argyll and the other refugees empowered James Stewart of Cultnes, a future Lord Advocate of Scotland, to write to William Carstares, another Scots dissident who had recently arrived in London, asking him to obtain money for the purchase of arms and ammunition from Lord Russell and his colleagues.[18] Robert Ferguson assisted him in his efforts. In the correspondence between London and the Continent their negotiations were hidden behind an elaborate cipher, in which Scotland is referred to as 'Brand' and England as 'Birch'. Argyll, once again, pressed for an advance of £30000 to enable him to mount an invasion of western Scotland. In addition, he asked for the support of 1000 horsemen, to be raised in the north of England, presumably from the estates of Lord Grey in Northumberland. When the time was right, it was intended that these men should ride to Edinburgh, while Argyll advanced from the west. Lord Russell, like Shaftesbury before him, baulked at Argyll's financial demands, suggesting that £10000 would be a more realistic sum. In the event, no money was ever raised, and no steps taken to assemble the cavalry Argyll had requested. Carstares soon tired of the English conspirators, whose amateurism and lack of determination contrasted so sharply with that of the Scots. Baillie of Jerviswood, who assisted Carstares in his negotiations, was to say in a clear mood of frustration

> that they had been too long the dupes of a set of men who could do nothing but talk: that this, however, was no reason why the Scots should desist: that, although there was but a small spark of liberty remaining in their country, it was still possible to blow it into a flame. If it was more difficult, it was likewise more honourable, to act independently of the English; and, if they were

successful, it would not be the first time England owed
its liberty to the interposition of Scotland.[19]

Matters now deteriorated to the point where Carstares
and his colleagues decided to press the English with an
ultimatum: unless they began to act with a greater sense
of urgency, all co-operation would be ended, and no further
steps taken to organise an insurrection in Scotland. No
reply was ever received, for the government was now
aware of the details of the Rye House Plot. Soon the
whole of the Whig underground, even those who had no
knowledge of Rumbold's plans, were under attack.

In June 1683, an oil merchant by the name of Josiah
Keeling, one of the minor conspirators, revealed the
details of the assassination plot and the more general
schemes for an insurrection to the authorities. In a mood
of panic, some of his colleagues gave themselves up. To
save their lives they turned King's Evidence, implicating
most of the Whig hierarchy. Russell, Grey, Sidney and
Essex were all arrested. Grey managed to escape, fleeing
to the continent, but the others were all sent to the Tower.
Essex committed suicide before his trial, but Russell and
Sidney were both judged and condemned, the former
dying in a particularly brutal fashion owing to the
incompetence of the executioner. Charles and James had
achieved their greatest political victory: the Whig party
had been dispersed and broken.

Rumbold managed to evade the general round-up,
taking refuge in Holland, where a community of political
exiles from both England and Scotland was steadily
growing in strength, including among their number
Robert Ferguson and Sir Thomas Armstrong, who also
evaded capture. Oddly enough, Rumbold, the republican
fanatic, and Argyll, the conservative nobleman, were

eventually to achieve a good understanding with each other. In 1685, Rumbold was to be one of Argyll's most loyal adherents and his best officer by far.

Argyll most certainly had no knowledge of the Rye House Plot, but the government uncovered his involvement in the wider Whig conspiracy at an early stage of the investigation. A number of his associates were arrested, including William Spence, his secretary, who was later tortured to extract information; even the Countess of Argyll and Lord Lorne were examined before the Privy Council. The interrogation of Spence was to provide a particularly rich source of new intelligence. A letter written by Argyll shortly before the discovery of the Rye House Plot was deciphered, giving the general direction of his thoughts, and his estimation of the strength of the government's forces in Scotland. His plans for aiding the Covenanter underground, and for seizing Edinburgh and Stirling castles were also revealed.[20] One thing was now certain: the house of Argyll would remain forfeit for as long as Charles and James were alive. Even Lord Lorne had been deprived of his title, innocent as he was, although for the sake of convenience we will continue to use it here. Monmouth, as heavily implicated as anyone in the general Whig plots, was as inconsistent and as muddle-headed as ever, at one point denouncing his co-conspirators, only to retract this denunciation once free of the court. He was initially protected by the continuing love of his father, although Charles was becoming increasingly exasperated by his erratic behaviour. He finally left for the continent in February 1684, after being summoned to give evidence in the forthcoming trial of John Hampden. Now in love with Lady Henrietta Wentworth, and free from the tutelage of Shaftesbury, he showed every sign of wishing to retreat from the limelight, waiting to be received back into his father's good graces. Sadly for him, neither fate nor Argyll was to allow him the peace he so earnestly desired.

In Holland, Argyll settled in a small estate in the province of Friesland, purchased some years before by his father, seemingly to provide a safe refuge. From here he made frequent visits to Amsterdam and Rotterdam. He also renewed his acquaintance with Ann Smith, who had a house in Utrecht. Religion was now playing a far greater part in his life than it had in the past, occupying much of the time left over from his political activities. There was also an active Presbyterian community in Holland, which had grown steadily since the 1660s. These men had contacts among the more extreme Covenanters in Scotland, but they were suspicious of the new exile, and there appears to have been little contact with him: hardly surprising considering the lack of real common ground between them.[20] Argyll did his best to maintain contact with Scotland, and received small sums of money from time to time. This was, however, hardly adequate to cover his present needs, so he was probably more dependent than ever on the generosity of Ann Smith and her indulgent husband. None of the money he was promised by his English co-conspirators was ever raised. One thing was obvious: Argyll could not remain in his present position indefinitely. The time for action had to come soon.

Enemy of the king

Over the next few months what is arguably the most open conspiracy in history gradually took shape. Many of the Whig exiles had concentrated in Holland, where British spies could closely observe their activities. The rebels were an odd collection of men: old soldiers of the New Model Army, as well as Whig aristocrats, republicans, troubled monarchists and extreme Presbyterians. Beyond hatred of James they had almost nothing in common, which ensured that their actions had little political coherence. They also appear to have held each other in deep suspicion. Robert Ferguson, as nefarious as ever, was soon to exercise his baleful influence over the impressionable Monmouth, who later described him as a 'bloody rogue, always advising the cutting of throats'.[1] Patrick Hume of Polwarth, the former associate of Shaftesbury, was much given to delivering long and tiresome speeches, the kind of tedious individual who never uses one word when twenty will do. His distrust of Argyll and his motives was to do much to undermine the whole enterprise. Andrew Fletcher of Saltoun, another Scot, was a skilled soldier and politician, and one of the few to urge caution, foreseeing that a hasty invasion of Britain would only end in disaster.

Increasingly impatient for action, Argyll seems to have given little thought to the fact that his former plans were now public knowledge, following the revelations of the Rye House Plot. By early 1684 he was already planning his return to Scotland. This came to nothing, owing to a shortage of funds, a problem that was finally remedied by Ann Smith and other sympathisers. With their help, he was able to stockpile arms and ammunition, using the cover that these were intended for export to Venice, which probably fooled very few.

In both London and Edinburgh, the British authorities were certainly well aware of Argyll's preparations. In May 1684, Charles ordered precautions taken against his planned invasion, informing the Privy Council of the Campbell chief's intentions to 'raise a considerable force in this our ancient kingdome'.[2] Orders for raising forces were issued to the lords lieutenant. In July, John Murray, Marquis of Atholl, Argyll's old enemy, was appointed Lord Lieutenant and Sheriff of Argyllshire by the Secret Committee of the Privy Council, acting as a ruling executive, and ordered to proceed immediately into the county with an armed force. Iain Lom was quick to welcome this.

Many a man with cuirass, fine gun and dark blue blade,
With their slender whingers supported by straps, such as
Lamont, Maclachlan, Macnaughton, Macdougall, Stewart
Of Appin, and Ewan of Lochaber, from the Black Wood
of Rannoch.

It is a matter of pride with you to be feared on
The eastside of Bonawe, although Campbells should exert

Themselves and seek protection of their swords; on your
Side is each person whom I have just mentioned, as
Unswervingly as an arrow; Macdonald from the strand will
Support you and the two Maclean chiefs.

Pluck the string harmoniously and do not cause the
Melodious strain to jar, do not unpropitiously keep your
Face turned to one whom you could not entrust your
Back, since the king has placed in the grasp of your hand
The scouring rod, and it was not of your asking, let it be
Time about with the blow, as hammers strike the anvil.[3]

The following month Atholl made his move, advancing
into the county with 1000 Highlanders, drawn from the
anti-Campbell clans mentioned in Iain Lom's poem. A
number of leading lairds were arrested, including
Campbell of Ardkinglas, suspected of corresponding with
his chief. Lord Neil Campbell, Argyll's brother, was also
arrested and only freed after pledging to remain loyal to
the government and persuade others to do the same.
Presbyterian ministers thought to be disloyal were deprived of their livings, and all those refusing to take the
Test were disarmed. In addition, Argyll's charter chest
was discovered and sent to the Secret Committee for
examination. Atholl remained for two months, making
sure that the county would not serve as a base of operations for the rebels, although generally acting with
moderation. On departing, he left Patrick Stewart of
Ballechin as his deputy, and placed a permanent garrison
in Inveraray Castle, which was to do much to frustrate
Argyll's designs the following year.[4] As well as awarding
Atholl's services by granting him the house, park and
mill of Inveraray, the Privy Council commended his
thoroughness and urged continuing vigilance: 'By what
is discovered in Argyll's papers since your parting ther is

ground for more and more rigorous prosecuting what may break of his hopes, and wee are confident your lordship will continue to end what you have so weell begunn.'[5]

Despite the best efforts of the Privy Council, the political situation remained generally tense. At the close of 1684, Fountainhall recorded something of the Shakespearean mood in Scotland.

> We ware troubled with the rumours of visions and apparitions, viz. a shower of blew bonnets seen in the air at Glasgow, and evanished when they came neir the ground. Item, a shower of blood at Moffat; and a little ghost and spectre appears at Rosneth, on my Lord Argile's houses, wher Athole has got his locality, and placed a garrison of 50 men; it beats the sojors sometimes, and bids them make good use of their tyme, for it shall not be long.[6]

The time came sooner than anyone could have predicted. In February 1685 Charles II died after a short illness. The Catholic James was now king.

For Monmouth, the death of Charles was a severe blow; in the place of an indulgent father came an unforgiving uncle. His hopes of being invited home were gone forever. Even before the death of the king, James had given instructions that the ports should be kept under close observation to prevent Monmouth entering England. Up to now, Monmouth seems to have played little part in the heated political games of his fellow exiles, and was even suspected of turning Catholic.[7] At this desperate time in his life he was prodded and poked into action by men who considered that it was vital to take action before the new regime was allowed to settle. In looking for its Lenin the Whig party turned to Argyll, who was soon urging a reluctant Monmouth into a joint invasion of Britain. A letter to William Spence, who had escaped from Scotland and was once again acting as Argyll's secretary, conveys something of the duke's mood at this time.

> You may well believe I have had time enough to reflect sufficiently upon our present state, especially since I came hither [to Rotterdam]. But whatever way I turn my thoughts, I find insuperable difficulties. Pray do not think it is an effect of melancholy, for that was never my greatest fault, when I tell you that in these three weeks retirement in this place, I have not only look'd back, but forward; and the more I consider our present circumstances, I think them still more desperate, unless some unforeseen accident fall out, which I cannot divine or hope . . . It's to me a vain argument, that our enemies are scarce well settled, when you consider that fear in some, and ambition in others, have brought them to comply . . . But that I may not seem obstinate in my own judgement, or neglect the advice of my friends, I will meet you at the time and place appointed. But for God's sake, think in the meantime of the improbabilities that lie naturally in our way; and let us not, by struggling with our chains make them straiter and heavier. For my part, I'll run the hazard of being thought anything, rather than a rash inconsiderate man. And to tell you my thoughts without disguise, I am now so much in love with the retir'd life, that I am never like to be fond of making a Bustle in the World again.[8]

Although Argyll had the drive, the determination and the money, his plan for an invasion of Scotland could only work if Monmouth launched a simultaneous attack on south-west England, where he had built up a considerable body of support in recent years. With Ferguson acting as an intermediary, the two men finally met in Rotterdam in early April. Argyll, pressing for action, said that he himself could expect to raise a large number of men in Scotland, both as chief of Clan Campbell and as the son of the Covenanter marquis.[9] He attempted to persuade Monmouth that, within a short time of landing, he would be master of all Scotland, if not prevented by forces from England. It was essential, therefore, that Monmouth's own rising keep time with that in Scotland.[10] The two men finally agreed that something had to be done before James was allowed to 'settle in Anti-christianism and tyranny at his pleasure'. But this was a rather vague conclusion to such an important meeting, and neither the military plans nor the political objectives of the proposed joint invasion were discussed in any detail.

It is almost certain that Argyll relied on some kind of diversion in his favour in the Covenanter Lowlands as well as England. He was encouraged in this by the large number of Presbyterian refugees in Holland, apparently willing to see in him the saviour of their cause. Included among these was William Cleland, who had composed the satire on the Highland Host and later fought with the Covenanters at Drumclog and Bothwell Brig; John Balfour of Burleigh, one of the assassins of Archbishop James Sharp, as well as the Revd George Barclay, who, like Cleland, had also been present at Bothwell Brig, and a number of other ministers. Yet considerable doubt must remain as to just how far Argyll could expect support in the Lowlands, for the picture had changed quite dramatically since the days of Lauderdale. In his historical notes, Sir John Lauder is sensitive to this transformation: 'Argile, minding the former animosities and discontents in the country, thought to have found us all alike combustible tinder, that had had no more adoe then to hold a match to us, and we would all blow up in rebellion: but the tymes are altered, and the people scalded so severly with the former insurrections, that they are frighted to adventure on a new on. '[11]

The policy of repression, briefly lifted with the third Indulgence, and then renewed with ever-greater severity, had the effect of fragmenting the Presbyterian opposition, forcing it to move in ever-decreasing circles. Although it may not have been entirely clear at the time, the rising of 1679, which ended in the Battle of Bothwell Brig, marks the high tide of the Covenanter resistance to the Restoration government. So, ironically, it was Monmouth who did much to ensure that the support that Argyll might have been expected to receive in the Lowlands failed to appear. What was left of the old spirit of defiance was no more than a hard core of fanatics, who considered Argyll, and virtually everyone else who did not share their views, as an enemy.

On 22 July 1680, just over a year after Bothwell Brig, the last serious attempt at an armed rising was easily defeated at Airds Moss in the valley of the River Ayr, where the Revd Richard Cameron was killed and his little army dispersed. Although implacable opponents of James, Cameron's followers, soon to be known as the Cameronians, formed a tiny minority among Presbyterian dissenters, refusing any compromise on the Covenants. More seriously from Argyll's point of view, they were also intensely sectarian; Argyll was remembered not as the son of the great marquis, but as the political ally of Lauderdale. Never at any time was he to express sympathy or support for the Covenants, which were not even mentioned in the Declaration he made at Campbeltown after his landing in Scotland. Lauder, continuing his observations on the lack of support for Argyll in the

87

Lowlands, notes: 'And these wild phanatiques in Galloway do ever still rail on him, as on who had brok ther Covenant and joined with the late King and his governors to oppresse them, and would have him first giving signes of his repentance, ere they concur with him.'[12]

In other words, they proposed to treat Argyll in much the same fashion as their fathers had treated Charles II in 1650, in circumstances much less favourable to their cause. Even William of Orange was later to be rejected by many of the Cameronians as an 'uncovenanted king'.

Failing to distinguish between religious moderates and political extremists, the government became ever more repressive in the period leading up to Argyll's arrival. Field executions, forever associated with the name of John Graham of Claverhouse, became commonplace in the early months of 1685, a period subsequently known as the Killing Times. With the opposition, beyond the Cameronian sects, largely broken in spirit, the government made assurance doubly assure by placing the main field army in the Lowlands when the crisis finally came. It is almost certain that if the rebels had landed there at the outset they would have faced a second Bothwell Brig, as Argyll himself suspected they might.[13]

For Argyll, the timing was vital. Helped by his financial backers, he had managed to gather a war chest of £10 000. With this he built up a small arsenal as well as hiring a number of Scots soldiers, who had been in the Dutch and German service. He was confident, moreover, that Clan Campbell would rise in strength as soon as he appeared in the Highlands. James could not be allowed to consolidate his hold on the throne; Argyll could not maintain his little army indefinitely, and the Dutch authorities were likely to cave in to English diplomatic pressure the longer they delayed. Although the authorities in Amsterdam, now the main base of operations, continued to be sympathetic, William of Orange, the leading although not the dominant figure in the Dutch Republic, ominously no longer treated his cousin Monmouth with the favour he had shown while Charles II was still alive, refusing to receive him at his little court. William was also James' son-in-law, the husband of his eldest daughter, Mary, and might also be expected to give way to family considerations.

On the threshold of the last great adventure of his life, it is important to ask what Argyll's political aims were. In the past Shaftesbury and the English Whigs had proposed Monmouth as an alternative to James, pushing the fiction of the 'black box'. Argyll, secure in his descent and pride of race, would have nothing to do with this nonsense. Before the enterprise got under way, Monmouth was made to promise that he would make no arbitrary claim to the throne. After Argyll landed in Scotland, his Declaration was published at Campbeltown; but this long and tedious document, written by the advocate James Stewart, is little more than a denunciation of Stewart misgovernment, providing few clues to Argyll's long-term thinking. Unlike some of his Scottish and English colleagues, we know that he was not a republican, and was unlikely to have welcomed a return of the Commonwealth. The most likely outcome is that James' Protestant daughter Mary, the heir apparent to the thrones of both England and Scotland, and her husband William of Orange, would have been invited over a few years before they eventually came. But the invasion was not a success; and in large measure the seeds of failure had been planted in Holland even before Argyll left.

One of the most important, if long-winded, sources for the 1685 rising is Patrick Hume's *Narrative of the*

Earl of Argyle's Expedition. Nevertheless, this document, written well after the event, has to be treated with some caution. Hume was, virtually from the outset, a political enemy of Argyll. All the failures of the expedition, according to Hume, can be laid at the feet of the earl, who neither listened to wisdom nor heeded advice; putting this in a slightly different way, he did his best to ignore Patrick Hume. But some of his stories are almost certainly inventions, including, for example, his assertion that Argyll, jealous of his own position, refused to allow Monmouth to accompany him to Scotland.[14] If he had there would have been no English rising, which Argyll, and others, recognised as vital to the success of the Scottish enterprise. Also the suggestion that Monmouth was put off from coming to Scotland because he was not used to fighting the kind of guerrilla warfare with which Argyll intended to open his campaign also seems to be a smokescreen; at no time did Argyll show any inclination to mount anything other than a conventional campaign. In the end, it has to be said that the prospects for a successful attack on Scotland, while never that good, were ruined to a significant degree by Hume himself.

Having gathered the men, money and material, and intending to raise his own clan for the cause, Argyll naturally assumed the leadership of the Scottish enterprise. But this immediately raised the suspicion of Hume and some of his colleagues, who believed that warfare was a business best managed by committees. At a meeting held in Rotterdam in April and attended by all the leading Scots conspirators, the matter came to a head. Almost from the outset, Argyll found his forecast of the likely support for a rising under close scrutiny. Irritated by this, and refusing to divulge the sources of his information, he lashed back, saying that if they would not trust him they could do as they pleased.[15] Sir John Cochran, the second son of the Earl of Dundonald, a far more diplomatic man than Hume, took the heat out of the situation by accepting Argyll's broad assurances.

When the question of leadership finally came up, Cochran immediately said that there was none so capable of command as the earl. Hume clearly disliked this, although he had neither enough status nor power to mount a direct challenge. Instead he drew on well-established Whig ideology. Argyll, he said, was certainly capable of being chosen to lead, not of assuming that leadership himself, for 'we are not for arbitrary power in what hand soever.'[16] In the end, presumably to urge on the endless proceedings, he was made to accept the leadership of the enterprise under the worst possible terms: 'I am resolved to doe nothing without the counsel of war, unless upon surprise, when there is no time to call a counsel; in which case any generall in the world acts by himself.'[17]

Argyll had in effect, taken a nominal command, for the council of war abrogated to itself all of the important details of military administration, including landing places, the appointment of officers, the raising of troops and the supervision of supplies. Argyll was only allowed to take the initiative when faced with a surprise attack. This was bad enough, but what was worse, no clear military objectives were agreed. Subsequent events make it clear that Argyll aimed to fight the campaign chiefly in his own Highlands, whereas Hume was determined that the army should proceed to the Covenanter Lowlands. He later claimed he had Monmouth's support for this strategy, but there is no evidence for this beyond his own word. This fundamental division was ultimately to paralyse the whole chain of command. Argyll's greatest error, as Lord Macaulay argues, is that he allowed himself to become a general in name alone.[18] It's only fair to add that he probably reckoned that once Clan Campbell had joined him in arms this would do much to stop the constant nagging of Hume and his colleagues.

It also has to be said that, in his eagerness to begin operations, Argyll was far too sanguine. In discussion with Cochran, he made a highly optimistic assertion. 'Doe you not think that the country where my interest is, being one of the best affected in Scotland, wher I have so many good relationes also well affected. Who albeit they should be inclined to ly at the first themselves . . . would certainly encourage ther people to joine, that my reckoning of 4 or 3000 is wide and improbable?'[19]

In this he failed to consider how far Atholl, recently reappointed Lord Lieutenant of Argyllshire, had weakened the military potential of his clan. Moreover, the Campbells were not quite the monolithic power bloc they had been in the past. Argyll's chief kinsman, John Campbell, Earl of Breadalbane, remained firmly on the side of the government. So too did Campbell of Cawdor, depriving him of the support he might be expected to receive from the people of Islay. More seriously, Argyll the rebel attracted to the side of the authorities the Macdonalds, Macleans, Camerons and the Appin Stewarts, all of the anti-Campbell clans who had served with Montrose, and were now poised to descend on the territory of their ancient enemy. Most serious of all, the success of the invasion depended on a closely co-ordinated attack on both Scotland and England. Monmouth, appointed to lead the English venture, promised Argyll that he would set out a few days after his own departure. In the event, he did not arrive on the Dorset coast until 11 June, by which time Argyll's venture was close to failure.

In London, James was kept closely advised on developments across the North Sea. In an audience with Arnold van Critters, the Dutch ambassador, he expressed his annoyance at the ambivalence of the authorities in Holland to the subversive activities of the émigrés. He also gave a clear indication whom he considered to be his greatest enemy – 'Of all men living Argyle has the greatest means of annoying me.'[20]

It is interesting to speculate on the attitude of the Dutch. Holland at this time was a decentralised republic, much like contemporary Switzerland. Local autonomy was jealously guarded, and even the Estates General, the Dutch parliament, could do little if opposed by the magistrates of Amsterdam or elsewhere. James' son-in-law, William of Orange, came from an old-established dynasty of Dutch aristocrats, and enjoyed the office of Stadholder – military leader – which had become virtually hereditary in his family. But even his power was of a limited nature, especially in peacetime. Amsterdam was a particularly good base for the rebels, because the local people were generally sympathetic and Robert Ferguson had good contacts with the magistrates. Even so, as James was perfectly well aware, the argument that the rebels were able to hide behind the constitution of the Dutch republic, used by Macaulay, can be taken too far. The communities of Holland were always able to act in concert when their security was threatened. In the past they had fought a long and heroic struggle for independence against Spain; now the great threat came from the France of Louis XIV. In the past, James had been sympathetic to an alliance with France. For Holland, the union of the two Catholic kings was a great strategic nightmare. Best then if James was kept preoccupied by a threat to the crown. William of Orange, far from being a helpless bystander, as Macaulay alleges, was playing a deep game, and made a financial contribution to the expenses of Argyll's invasion.[21] He probably reckoned that Argyll and Monmouth would make a better showing than they eventually did, keeping James preoccupied for the foreseeable future. But neither he, nor the Estates General, nor the magistrates of Amsterdam could maintain the pretence forever, adding to Argyll's sense of urgency.

With the aid of James Delap, a Scottish factor in Rotterdam, Argyll purchased three ships – the thirty-gun *Anna*, the twelve-gun *David* and the six-gun *Sophia*. All three were anchored at Vlie, the old passage from the Zuyder Zee to the North Sea, lying between Vlieland and Torschelling. When Argyll and his colleagues arrived from Amsterdam on 28 April only the *David* was loaded and ready to sail; it was to take another two days for the remaining ships to be ready, causing Argyll acute nervous anxiety. Bevil Skelton, the English ambassador, had himself observed the little flotilla, and was known to be making representations at The Hague.[22] According to Hume, Argyll is said to have considered sailing before the necessary documentation had been obtained, and under the guns of a nearby warship. He was persuaded to drop this rash suggestion, although he took temporary refuge on the *David*.

There was a mood of great anticipation that spring. In Rotterdam, some Scots skippers heard of the preparations and later reported that 'the Scots Ministers ther prayed for the good successe of ther navy imployed in the cause of God'.[23] Among the exiled Presbyterians the venture was likened to a 'Holy Warre'. Some of the ministers preached with such success that wives urged their husbands to enlist. John Holwell, a kind of English

Nostradamus, had published not many years before a
book of prophecy by the title of *Catastrophe Mundi*. One
of the illustrations showed a little Highland man brandishing a sword over a field of dead bodies, which some
took to be Argyll. Finally, at 7 p.m. on 2 May, urged on
by prayer and prediction, the three ships set sail. The
Dutch, who had one of the most powerful fleets in
Europe, all too late made a last minute gesture to appease
James. A yacht was sent out from Amsterdam, the captain
later reporting that he found all three ships under way
and falling back after he was fired upon.[24]

In all there were some three 300 men on board, including Argyll's younger sons, Charles and John. His eldest,
Archibald, Lord Lorne, was in London at the time, even
offering to take up arms against his father, but he was
later imprisoned in the Tower on suspicion of 'dangerous
practices'. To emphasise the nature of the joint enterprise,
Argyll was accompanied by two Englishmen – Richard
Rumbold and John Ayloffe, another old officer of the
New Model Army. Andrew Fletcher of Saltoun, who was
highly sceptical about the prospects for success, remained
in Holland, later accompanying his friend Monmouth
to England, as did Robert Ferguson. Some, including
William Cleland and George Barclay, had been sent
ahead to gather intelligence and assess the prospects for
a rising in the Lowlands.

William Veitch, who had aided Argyll's escape in 1681,
was sent to Northumberland, with a commission from
Lord Grey, instructing his steward to provide money and
men to support the rising north of the border, a strategy
agreed in outline some years before. It is uncertain if
Lord Grey's tenants, who never at any time showed any
rebellious inclination, would have obeyed his orders. In
the end it came to nothing, because the authorities were

soon aware of Veitch's presence, forcing him to take refuge in the wilds of Reidsdale. George Pringle of Torwoodlee, another agent, was sent to Moray in north-west Scotland, where Argyll had some connections, and the prospect of a diversionary raid had been discussed; but this was not fertile territory for the rebels and nothing came of the proposal.

Back on board the *Anna*, Argyll suggested that he would sail with the *David*, as she needed the presence of a person of 'note and discretion', seemingly little more than a convenient cover to get away from the verbose Hume. Cochran insisted that he should remain in the admiral's ship, offering to make the transfer himself. Argyll refused to be parted from him, whereupon Hume agreed to go, no doubt to the relief of all. Before leaving, he made his parting shot, insisting that the council of war be called at regular intervals throughout the voyage, when the weather permitted. Argyll was now crossing his own personal Rubicon; there was no going back.

7

The fiery cross

In Scotland, the government had been expecting Argyll's arrival for some time. As early as 12 April reports had been received that he was already at sea with 4000 men.[1] Scotland was put in a state of defence. Among other things, the Privy Council ordered the imprisonment of Countess Anna, Argyll's wife, who was taken to Edinburgh Castle. Lady Sophia Lindsay was also placed under arrest, and held in the far less salubrious Tolbooth, the common jail, a spiteful act to repay her for helping Argyll escape in 1681. Lord Neil, Argyll's brother, and James, his youngest son, were also taken in this general round-up of the leading Campbells. When parliament assembled in late April, a message was read out from the new king.

> Nothing hes been left unattempted by those wild and inhumane traitors for endeavouring to overturn your peace; and therfor We have good reason to hope, that nothing will be wanting in you to secure yourselves and

Us from their outrages and violence in time coming, and
to take care that such conspirators meet with their just
deservings, so that others may be deterred from courses
so little agreeable to Religon, or their dutie and allegiance
to Us.[2]

In preparing for the invasion, the authorities had been
reasonably thorough. Atholl, Breadalbane, and the Duke
of Gordon were all empowered to raise local forces. Irish
troops were brought to the coast of Ulster, ready to be
transported to Scotland in case of need, and regular forces
began to congregate in the Lowlands under George
Douglas, Earl of Dumbarton, the commander-in-chief
in Scotland. Ironically, Dumbarton, a Catholic, had been
allowed to assume his command without taking the Test.

Interestingly, preparations in Argyllshire itself were less
than adequate. Atholl did not arrive at Inveraray until
30 May. In his absence, Patrick Stewart was left to defend
the county with only 500 men. It seems reasonably certain
that the authorities were more worried by the prospect
of the Lowlands rising for Argyll than his own clan, much
of which had previously been neutralised by the actions
of Atholl. Part of Dumbarton's force was positioned to
prevent a landing on the Ayrshire coast, and serious
attempts were made to stamp out the last vestiges of
Covenanter resistance.

Argyll's voyage was favoured by the weather; early on
the morning of 5 May the Aberdeenshire coast was
sighted as it enters the Moray Firth.[3] The following day
they arrived in the Orkneys. Then things started to go
wrong: the winds died away, followed by the onset of a
thick fog. Uncertain of the waters, the seamen missed
the passage between the Orkneys and the Shetlands,
finally taking refuge in the evening in the great harbour

of Scapa Flow, on the southern shore of Mainland, the largest of the Orkneys. Unable to proceed further, anchor was dropped in Swanbister Bay, where it was decided to send a party ashore to seek pilots to guide them out of the fog. William Spence, who had an uncle living in Kirkwall, the Orkney capital, and William Blackadder, the son of the Covenanter preacher, volunteered for the task, promising to return the next day with as many recruits as they could find. Argyll seemingly gave them permission to proceed as far as Kirkwall, presumably hoping to gain good intelligence from Spence's uncle, without troubling to consult the council of war. It seems certain that, highly resentful of the importunities of Hume, the earl decided to act on his own initiative. If so, it was to be a disastrous decision, and probably did much to weaken his authority still further. In a small place like Kirkwall it was almost impossible to keep the presence of strangers hidden. That same evening the two men were arrested on the orders of the local bishop and magistrates as 'servants to a rebel'.[4] News of rebel presence was at once sent to Edinburgh.

By the following day Argyll and his colleagues learned of this small disaster. There is no reason to assume that the council of war would have acted with any greater wisdom than Argyll and refused permission for Spence and Blackadder to go to Kirkwall, but the fact that it was not consulted, contrary to the Amsterdam agreement, immediately placed Argyll on the defensive. He began to backtrack, saying that he had only given permission for them to go ashore, not to Kirkwall. The loss of Spence would have been a particularly severe blow. As Argyll's secretary he was in possession of much important information, which, as before, would doubtless be tortured out of him. More seriously, it was an early blow to the

morale of the expedition. The advantage of surprise, arguably the only ace the rebels held, had now been completely lost. There is also a wider point to be considered:
Orkney, as Argyll must have known, was not fertile
territory for the rebel cause. At no time did the local
people show any sympathy for the Covenanters, and had
adjusted quite happily to the Episcopalian system. But
even if they had reacted sympathetically to the arrival of
the rebels, the islands were too far from the centre of
power to make any real difference to the outcome of the
struggle. Any advantage gained would, in other words,
have been more than offset by the intelligence gained by
the authorities.[5]

To try and recover from the disaster, Hume suggested
that an attack be made on Kirkwall. This was not considered practicable because the town was too well
defended. Neither Argyll nor Hume nor anyone else
wished to get bogged down in the Orkneys. It was vital
that the matter delayed their onward progress as little as
possible. On Argyll's suggestion, it was agreed that an
armed party be sent ashore to seize some of the local
gentry to be used in a possible prisoner exchange. In all,
five men were unfortunate enough to be caught up in
the rebel sweep, including one James Stewart, the Laird
of Graemesay.[6] Before leaving Amsterdam the rebels had
apparently been told by an astrologer that they were
destined to capture a James Stewart of the blood royal,
which must have given some small comfort to those who
believed in that sort of thing. The prophecy proved to be
accurate; but certainly not in the way imagined. The
Laird of Graemesay declared himself to be a descendant
of the Earl of Orkney, a bastard son of James V.[7] His
capture appears to have made very little difference to the
bishop, who quickly called Argyll's bluff, making no reply

to his letter demanding a prisoner exchange. Unable to delay any longer, the flotilla sailed on to the Hebrides, taking the Orcadians with them, together with a small supply ship captured in Swanbister Bay.

On Monday 11 May the three ships anchored in the bay of Tobermory. The winds that favoured Argyll's passage on his southwards voyage through the Hebrides acted against the Royal Navy, coming from the Irish Sea, and it remained absent for several important days.

From the anchorage at Tobermory, Argyll sent his son Charles to the mainland of Lorne to summon his vassals to meet him in arms. Charles managed to take possession of the old stronghold of Dunstaffnage Castle and sent a rider bearing the fiery cross through the countryside, an ancient Celtic device used by chiefs to raise their clans, with the news that *MacCailen Mor* had come home. He also sent out letters from his father to the leading gentry. Contrary to all of Argyll's expectations, the response was at best lukewarm, and at worst treacherous. Some were in prison; others cowed into submission and still others loyal to the king. Campbell of Lochnell promised his support, only to forward Argyll's letter to the Privy Council. In all, Charles managed to assemble only 200 volunteers at this first summons. Still, at least he managed to secure the promise of support of Sir Duncan Campbell of Auchinbreck, the most powerful laird in the area, and a garrison was put in Carnasserie Castle and the small town of Ederline was occupied.[8]

Because it was destined to collapse so quickly, it is often said that Argyll's adventure was foredoomed.[9] This, however, is not an accurate reading of the circumstances of the time. The government was certainly well prepared, and had many more troops in arms than Argyll himself estimated, but there was still considerable uncertainty as to where the main blow would fall. James appears to have been convinced, following Hume's mental process, that the rebels were bound to attempt a link up with the Covenanters of Ayrshire and Galloway. The defence of the Highlands was left, for the most part, to the irregular troops raised by Atholl, Breadalbane and the other loyal noblemen. Even some of these men, including some 300 raised by Breadalbane, were taken away to the south-west. More seriously, the government had insufficient supplies to maintain those who were left for more than a few weeks.[10] All that Argyll had to do was to score some early successes, which could easily have allowed him to maintain himself in the western Highlands until such time as Monmouth appeared in England. Breadalbane was clearly aware of this danger, writing to Patrick Stewart of Ballechin, Atholl's deputy, pointing out that Argyll was looking for a quick military advantage, urging, 'for God's sake disappoint him.'[11]

We know from hindsight that Argyll was an uninspiring soldier. At the time, though, he was an unknown quantity, who at least had some experience of warfare in the Highlands. At the height of his success he assembled less than 2000 men, but Montrose had an army not much stronger when he won some of his famous battles. Unbeknown to Breadalbane, however, the loyalists possessed an important advantage. Montrose had Alasdair MacColla; Argyll had Patrick Hume. He and his supporters constantly undermined the earl's authority, insisting on a descent on the Lowlands, regardless of the military realities. This, and Argyll's own lack of personal determination, were set to ruin the campaign.

Many others shared Breadalbane's sense of unease. News of Argyll's landing caused widespread anxiety.[12] In the early days, the mood of panic spread as far as the

Secret Committee of the Privy Council, leading to one of their most savage orders. Atholl was instructed to 'destroy what you can to all who joynd, and are not come off on your or Breadalbane's advertisement, are to be killed, or disabled ever from fighting again; and burn all houses except honest men's, and destroy Inverarra and all the castles; and what you cannot undertake, leeve to those who comes after you to do . . . let the women and children be transported to remote isles.'[13]

Atholl, to his credit, behaved with far greater moderation than these instructions allowed. There is, however, an interesting thought-process at work here. In dealing with Highland problems, the Lowland authorities, as far back as the reign of James V, had considered adopting extreme measures. For most of the Restoration period, the religious dissidents of south-west Scotland had caused repeated problems; but there was never any suggestion that the solution to this lay in wholesale murder and transportation. Highlanders, in contrast, even the traditionally loyal Campbells, could be perceived as savages and thus treated in a savage way. Not many years from the events of 1685, this murderous intent was to fall on the little community living in the shadows of Glencoe.

Charles' news from Lorne was a serious disappointment to his father, hoping for a much more wholehearted support from his kin. As Breadalbane recognised, he needed an early victory to give momentum to the rising, and to bring an end to the criticism of Hume. The opportunity for this came with the news that Patrick Stewart was on Islay, disarming the local population, with the help of Hugh Campbell, Cawdor's bailie. Argyll, who had hopes of raising 600 men on the island, decided to surprise Stewart. Charles was left behind in Lorne, presumably helping Auchinbreck raise his tenants, while the flotilla sailed south, past the hostile garrison in Duart Castle, making for the narrows between Islay and Jura. Once anchored off Port Askaig on the east of Islay, Argyll landed his troops under cover of night, then marching south-west to Killarow – now Bowmore – where Stewart was reported to be.[14] Seemingly forewarned, Stewart managed to escape before the enemy arrived, making his way to Kintyre with all the serviceable arms. It was to be a feature of the whole campaign that the government forces, although equal and sometimes superior to those of Argyll, continually evaded the insurgents to deny them the prospect of any advantage.

Although the people of Islay were generally well disposed to the rebel cause, some even taking to the hills rather than taking the oath of allegiance forced on them by Stewart, surprisingly few volunteered to join the rising. Instead of the 600 Argyll hoped for, only eighty came forward, and many of these were soon to desert. His hopes were in large measure frustrated by the local gentry, loyal to Cawdor, who unanimously refused their support. Argyll even resorted to threatening to hang Hugh Campbell unless more recruits came forward, but this was another bluff, no more successful than that made in the Orkneys. Apart from Charles and Auchinbreck, Argyll's last remaining hope now lay with the Presbyterian communities of southern Kintyre. From Port Askaig he sailed onwards, arriving at Campbeltown on Wednesday 20 May.

Argyll had probably always intended to use Campbeltown, far from any immediate threat of danger, as his main base of operations. It was here, so to speak, that he raised his standard, and did his best to define the political aims of the rising. The Declaration, composed in The Netherlands by James Stewart, was read out at the Market Cross, reminding the audience of the many injustices of

Stewart rule, right back to the execution of the earl's father in 1661.[15] James, only ever referred to as the Duke of York, was denounced as a 'bigot papist', the leading representative of the 'hellish Mystery of Antichristian Iniquity and arbitrary Tirannie', which made such advances in the reign of the late king. It was implied, moreover, that he was responsible for the murder of his brother, a rumour widespread at the time. But the document was curiously negative, saying little that was not already familiar to those with receptive ears. James, seemingly, was to be brought down on a wave of Protestant anger against a Catholic king. Who, or even what, was to come in his place receives no mention. No appeal was made to the Covenants, which may have inspired the more fanatical Presbyterians, but would surely have alienated everyone else, especially in England. What could be said, and what, was said, was effectively dictated by the negative nature of Whig politics, whose only constant feature was hatred of James. In effect, the revolution Argyll proposed was one of the most unusual in history: it had to be taken on trust alone. Some of Monmouth's advisors were eventually to recognise this obvious political weakness. After he landed in England, and contrary to his promise to Argyll, he declared himself the rightful successor to Charles II.

Soon after the reading of this public statement, Argyll made a more personal statement. In this he implied, in so many words, that he had not been the best of debtors, and promised, once restored to his just rights, to satisfy not only his own debts but also those of his father, something he had resisted in all the years of his power. This appears to have had at best a limited impact; most of those to whom he owed money probably never learned of his promise, and are not likely to have been moved by it, even if they had. Both of these documents were subsequently published in a mobile printing press that Argyll had brought along with him from Holland, together with a Dutch compositor, showing he had an early appreciation of the importance of propaganda and spin. The unfortunate man who printed the two Declarations later fell captive, falling back on the defence that he spoke no English and thus had no idea what the documents contained.

The need for recruits was now more desperate than ever, as only twelve men remained from the Islay volunteers. Although, as expected, a sufficient number of people came forward from Campbeltown and the surrounding areas to be organised into three companies, their loyalty was to the Protestant cause rather than Argyll as such, and probably did more to strengthen the hand of Hume and the Lowlanders against the beleaguered general. Still lacking sufficient numbers, the rebels were reduced to sending press gangs throughout the rest of Kintyre, forcing a number of men into service, later used in appeals for clemency.[16]

Something of Argyll's increasingly anxious mood can be detected in a letter he wrote to the Laird of Loup at Campbeltown on 22 May appealing for support, and probably similar to many others of the same kind:

> It hath pleased God to bring me safe to this place, where several of both nations doth appear with me for the defence of the Protestant religion, our Lives and Liberties, against Popery and Arbitrary Government, whereof the Particulars are in two Declarations emitted by those noble-men, Gentle-men and others and by me for my self. Your father and I lived in great friend-ship, and I am glad to serve you his son in the Protestant Religion, and

I will be ready to do it in your particular when there is occasion. I beseech you let not any out of fear or other bad principles perswade you to neglect your Duty to God and your Countrey at this time, or believe that D. York is not a Papist, or that being one, he can be a righteous King. Then know that all England is in arms in several places and the Duke of Monmouth appears at the same time upon the same grounds we do, and few places in Scotland but soon will joyn, and the South and West waits but till they hear I am landed, for so we resolved before I left Holland. Now I beseech you make no delay to separate from those who abuse you, and are carrying on a Popish design, and come with all the men of your command to assist the Cause of Religion, where you shall be most welcome to.[17]

The reference to Monmouth is little more than political bait, for Argyll had no hard information on the duke's whereabouts at this time. In keeping with the agreed plan, he should have been in England. However, lack of money kept him in Holland longer than expected, and he was not ready to leave until two days after Argyll's letter. Even then, he was prevented from sailing for several more days by adverse weather. Fighting against the winds, it took him twelve days to make the relatively short passage from the Texel to Dorset, where he landed at Lyme Regis on 11 June. Before his death, Argyll was to blame the late arrival of Monmouth for the failure of the Scottish rising.[18] This is almost certainly untrue. Even if Monmouth had left as planned, its unlikely to have made any real difference. Both emergencies were largely self-contained, and no English troops were called on to serve in Scotland.

At Campbeltown, the new volunteers were organised under colours bearing the mottoes 'For the Protestant

Religion' and 'Against Popery, Prelacy, and Erastianism'.
Arms were distributed and officers appointed. Argyll's
problem was to be just the opposite of Monmouth's: he
had too many officers and not enough foot soldiers. Only
the most experienced received early command, regardless
of nationality: Richard Rumbold was given a colonelcy
in the cavalry, and his fellow countryman, John Ayloff, a
nephew by marriage of Argyll's old enemy the Earl of
Clarendon, was given a similar commission in one of the
foot regiments. Some of the others, however, were
seriously under-employed, probably adding to their
general sense of frustration. No sooner were the details
of military administration settled than Hume began his
incessant demand for an immediate descent on the
Lowlands. He was encouraged in this by a report received
from George Barclay that the people in Carrick were ready
to rise, and that 1000 horse would join the insurgents
within a few days of landing, and 2000 infantry would
follow on. Barclay went on to claim that the enemy were
in a state of panic, some of their troops locking themselves
up in the castle at Glasgow, that Monmouth was in
England with a great army and his proclamation had
already reached Ayr.[19] Encouraged by this, Hume even
proposed dividing the small army, at this time probably
no more than 600 men, and taking half over to Ayrshire.

John Willcock, Argyll's biographer, argues that this was
the best course of action, which, if followed, might have
given the history of the invasion a quite different
outcome.[20] It's difficult to accept the logic behind this
contention. Willcock goes on to say that Barclay's statement about Monmouth was a baseless rumour. More
than this, it was an outright lie. There is no reason,
therefore, to accept his assertion that thousands of men
were ready to take to arms. It gives all the appearance of

being little more than wishful thinking. Beyond the exaggerated expectations of those in alliance with Hume, there is virtually no evidence of any widespread support for the rebels in the Lowlands, still well policed by government troops. For Argyll to divide his small force at this time would have been quite disastrous; it would also have meant turning his back on Charles and Auchinbreck, who had managed to collect a reasonably impressive force of 1200 Campbells further to the north at Tarbert.

On the general's insistence, the army moved north by land and sea, following in the wake of yet another fiery cross. Meeting at Tarbert on 27 May the combined rebel force came to about 1800 men, well under what Argyll had predicted. Still, with the military supplies he had brought from Holland, they were well equipped and could be expected to make a good showing against the weaker royal forces in the area. By far the best prospect for success was offered by an immediate attack on Inveraray, held at this stage only by Patrick Stewart and his small force. If the Campbell capital fell it would probably have had a great effect on the demoralised clan. Even if Atholl attacked, he could be delayed by an effective use of guerrilla tactics, until such time as the tardy Monmouth arrived in England, which would have given the whole enterprise a considerable boost. Besides, the Campbell soldiers are unlikely to have agreed to embark on any adventure in the Lowlands until their own homes were first secured. Richard Rumbold, Argyll's most experienced officer, give his support to the commander's strategy. However, the advance on Tarbert was as much as the Lowland gentry were prepared to tolerate. At once the debating club was set in motion, undermining the earl's authority, and demanding an immediate descent on the Lowlands.

For any commanding officer even one mutinous subordinate is a danger to the good order of the army; Argyll was faced with a multitude. In the circumstances this was catastrophic. It clearly had an effect on the morale of the army, for many of the Highlanders, distrusted and disliked by their Lowland comrades, soon began to desert. It most certainly had an affect on Argyll's own morale and sense of self-esteem. At the conclusion of his dismal adventure he was to express his feelings with some bitterness:

> Those who went with me kept constant cabals, sent messengers, received intelligence by themselves, acquainted me but with what they pleased, and were trepanned by spies sent by the enemy; and to the last hour never got one intelligence of use, nor assured me of one man to join with me; and when they spake or sent to any, did it in their own name. Once they persuaded me, like a fool, to give a letter of trust to one they sent out, and, like a raven he never returned. They designed sometimes to have seized ships, arms and provisions, and effectually did break open, use, and embezzle what they pleased, without me. Some of them lived riotously, and spent the provisions as they pleased, so that many arms were spoiled and many lost, and provisions were spent sooner than was necessary; and except two hundred ducatoons I left, I spent all the silver upon them, and they claimed all as their due.[21]

Clearly this statement has to be treated with as much caution as Hume's *Narrative*, as Argyll was looking to excuse himself and blame others. However, while the details may be suspect, the essential truth is not. Lacking firm direction and command, the rebel army drifted on the Highland fringe like a rudderless ship. Faced with the hostility and opposition of his colleagues, and his strategy subject to endless analysis, Argyll appears to have been gripped at Tarbert by a kind of intellectual paralysis. At one stage he proposed dividing the army, along the lines previously suggested by Hume, retaining the Highlanders for his attack on Inveraray, while allowing the rest of the army to sail in the *Sophia* for the coast of Ayrshire. No sooner was this agreed than he changed his mind, causing Sir John Cochran to remark that he would go to Ayrshire regardless, alone if necessary and armed only with a pitchfork. Soon a decision was forced on the earl: unable to advance into the Highlands, and faced with the prospect of widespread disaffection, he had no choice but to abandon the attack on Inveraray. The constant delays were also eating up the army's supplies. To resolve the problem, it was decided to cross from Tarbert to the Isle of Bute. Lacking adequate transport, it was to take three days before the whole force completed the crossing. Time was now most definitely on the side of the king.

8

The devil and the deep blue sea

The whole time the Campbell army remained at Tarbert, in a position of relative strength, was an anxious one for the government. It was feared that the rebels would make an early descent on Inveraray before reinforcements arrived. Atholl appears to have even considered making a withdrawal, ordering Stewart to burn the town and remove all provisions, arms and ammunition. Breadalbane was also instructed to assist him if he got into difficulties, by 'sending a pertie of your menne you trust mos to bring of Ballechan if he be in heasert'.[1] Bit by bit the position began to improve. On Bute the rebels were poised for an attack on either the Highlands or the Lowlands, but at least the pressure was off Patrick Stewart. Soon government reinforcements were arriving at Inveraray in ever-increasing numbers. Atholl himself came on 30 May. More important still, the Royal Navy, headed by the frigate HMS *Kingfisher*, had sailed into the Firth of Clyde in some strength. To mark its presence, Captain Thomas Hamilton of the *Kingfisher* attacked and destroyed Carrick Castle, the old Campbell stronghold on Loch Goil. News of this reached Argyll on Bute. He responded by ordering that Rothesay Castle, once the favourite residence of the Stewart kings, be set alight, in a rather futile act of reprisal. Hamilton, now stationed at Dumbarton, was told to be on the alert for enemy fire-ships, although no attack of this kind ever appears to have been contemplated.[2]

Although the rebels hoped for support as well as supplies on Bute, their presence seems to have been little more than a nuisance. The gathering of supplies was a legitimate if unwelcome act of war; but some of the army, especially the Highlanders, began widespread looting, even breaking into the poor box in the parish church of Rothesay.[3] Charles Campbell, some of whose men were responsible for these outrages, seems to have been publicly rebuked by the local minister.

It is clear from his actions on Bute that Argyll still had no clear strategy, doing little beyond ordering probes of the nearby shores. Hume and Cochran were allowed to take a small party of sixty men off on a reconnaissance of the Ayrshire coast, while Charles crossed over to the nearby Cowal Peninsula on yet another recruiting drive. Landing on the island of Great Cumbrae, the Lowlanders discovered that the town of Largs on the adjacent mainland was strongly held by a large force of government cavalry and infantry. All they could do was gather boats for future use, but no sooner had they left than enemy soldiers arrived on the island and promptly staved them in. Back on Bute, Hume continued to bicker with Argyll, apparently having learned nothing from his experience at Largs. On Cowal, Charles Campbell fared even worse, suffering the most serious setback to date. No sooner had he and his men left their boats than they came under attack by a party of government soldiers, commanded Captain Kenneth Mackenzie of Suddie. In the firefight that followed, the rebels began to run short of ammunition. Charles immediately returned to the boats to order more to be brought forward. In doing so, he appears to have given no clear directions, for his men assumed he was running away and were quick to follow his example. In the undignified flight back to the shore some were killed and others taken prisoner. The remainder took refuge on the castle of Eilean Dearg, yet another old Campbell fortification, situated on a small island in Loch Riddon, just to the north of Bute. Once the danger was past, they rejoined the main army. To try to compensate for this blow to morale, Argyll decided to cross in strength to Castle Toward, on the easternmost prong of the Cowal trident, planning to remove all enemy forces in the area. He was free to do so without being criticised because Hume and Cochran had sailed off in early June in the *Sophia* and *David,* along with another small vessel by the name of *Francis,* to attempt yet another probe on the mainland.[4]

Avoiding Largs and the Ayrshire coast, they dropped anchor further north opposite the little port of Greenock. Here they discovered that the shore was held by a troop of enemy cavalry under the command of Lord Cochran. In attempting to overcome this obstacle, Hume received some of the broth he had been steadily laying out to Argyll. One of the officers, Robert Elphinston of Orkney, objected that it was too dangerous to attempt a forced landing under enemy fire, refusing even to obey orders to make the attempt. Lord Macaulay reports this as simple cowardice. John Willcock makes the rather peculiar defence of Elphinston's conduct by saying that that it was scarcely possible to keep discipline among a company of gentlemen adventurers – which seems to be the essential weakness of the whole Argyll Rising – and he was right to see the endeavour as dangerous![5] That Elphinston did indeed lack backbone was to be amply demonstrated by his later conduct.

On Elphinston's refusal to make the attempt, command of the landing party was given to one Major John Fullarton. As they approached the shore they came under enemy fire, whereupon the *Sophia* and the *David* responded with their bigger guns. Lord Cochran promptly fell back, allowing Fullarton and his twelve men to make an unopposed landing. The two sides entered into a parley, during which John Huston, Cochran's second-in-command, objected to the invasion. In response, Fullerton said that 'they were come to their native country, for the preservation of the Protestant religion, and the liberties of the country, and it was a pity that brave gentlemen should appear against them, in the service of the popish tyrant and usurper.'[6] Tempers flared and Huston fired his pistol, to which Fullarton and his men immediately responded. By this time, however, more men had landed, and, once again under fire from the ships, Lord Cochran and his party rode off in the direction of Paisley.

Sir John Cochran and Patrick Hume were among those who came ashore, where, contrary to all their exaggerated expectations, they found the local people far from enthusiastic. In all only thirty men volunteered to join the rising, and only after they had been formally pressed to protect their families from any reprisals. Instead of the two hundred bolls of meal they expected for the sustenance of the army, Hume and Cochran managed to gather only forty. Hume then sailed back to join Argyll on Cowal, soon to show that he had, once again, learned absolutely nothing.

Argyll, clearly frustrated by the setbacks suffered to date, was now determined to make a fresh attempt on Inveraray, under far less favourable circumstances than before. Even then, Hume, despite his setback at Greenock, raised objections, insisting that the council of war be summoned. Argyll, understandably, lost his temper, falling, as Hume reports, into a 'great passion'. Recovering his composure, he asked for a 24-hour delay, after which he would lay his plans before the council.[7] In the meantime, he went off to inspect the castle of Eilean Dearg. As Argyll was by now very well aware, the rebels had lost the freedom of the seas, and, as yet, still had no secure supply base or anchorage. With the English frigates now close to the Kyles of Bute it was vital that some emergency action was taken. On his return, he immediately suggested using the old castle as a store for the arms and ammunition, the constant transport of which must surely have hampered the army's mobility. The ships, moreover, should be anchored in Loch Riddon, just to the north of Eilean Dearg. These waters were considered too dangerous (mistakenly, as it turned out) to allow the approach of the larger enemy vessels. For once, the council of war decided in Argyll's favour against the opposition of Hume, swung in this direction, no doubt, by Sir John Cochran, who no longer considered it advisable to make an immediate landing in the Lowlands. Some of Hume's associates suggested to him that they might seize the vessels, regardless of the council's decision. He persuaded them against this, but Argyll, clearly sensing mutiny, made doubly sure by stationing some of his Highlanders on each of the ships.[8]

Argyll's flotilla, now augmented by smaller supply ships taken since his arrival in Scotland, made its way through the Kyles of Bute into Loch Riddon. Once there, the surplus stores were removed to the castle, which was further protected by the construction of a small earthen rampart on the western side, armed with some of the four- and five-pounders brought from the ships. These guns, of course, were no match for the thirty-pounders of the Royal Navy, as Hume points out in his *Narrative*. As always, he appears to have been wise after the event. In any case, the rebel ships took up their more secure anchorage only just in time; for the *Kingfisher*, with the support of the *Falcon*, the *Mermaid* and the *Charlotte*, was now cruising close to the Kyles of Bute. News of Argyll's new position soon reached the Privy Council, which concluded that he had abandoned his amphibious campaign, and was likely to aim at taking the important stronghold of Dumbarton, or even Stirling in central Scotland. To prevent this, the Edinburgh militia was ordered to march 'tho it war Sunday'.[9]

Now cut off from the sea, Argyll attempted to secure the landward approach to the north of his base against a possible attack by Atholl. Rumbold, heading the cavalry, was sent on a sweep through Glendaurel, followed by a body of infantry led by Major Henderson. Acting with courage and determination, Rumbold rode as far north as Ardkinglas Castle, on the shores of Loch Fyne across from Inveraray, even managing to take the stronghold. All of Atholl's counter attacks were held off until Argyll arrived with the main body. Although Atholl had considerably more men than Argyll, he adhered to strict Fabian tactics, refusing to allow the enemy any opportunity of seizing the initiative, a cautious approach that caused intense frustration to Sir Ewan Cameron, the chief of the Camerons of Locheil, and was later to lead to accusations of incompetence. But it worked. Seeing the enemy could not be teased out of the camp at

Inveraray, the Lowlanders demanded a return to the south.

Trapped between the royal army to the north and the navy to the south, the rebels, as Atholl put it, were in 'perfyt hose nett'.[10] On 9 June, Patrick Stewart wrote to the Marchioness of Atholl in a mood of growing confidence, saying that Argyll had little option left but to make some attempt to advance westwards, possibly in the direction of Stirling. There is little doubt that the government now fully aware how weak the pulse of the rebellion really was. 'I think,' Stewart reports 'a few days will ane end to this Affair.'[11] Even so, the Secret Committee was taking no chances, instructing Atholl to do nothing in haste. The marquis was not without his own problems at this time. The day before Argyll arrived at Ardkinglas, Cameron of Locheil's men had attacked some of the Perthshire gentry in the mistaken belief that they were rebel soldiers. Half a dozen or so were killed before the mistake was discovered.[12] Even after the matter had been settled, Locheil continued to be held in some suspicion, as were the Breadalbane Campbells and, surprisingly, the Macleans, no doubt adding still further to Atholl's sense of caution.

Atholl's problems, of course, were as nothing compared to those of Argyll. Uncertain what to do for the best, he suggested that the flotilla, now closely blockaded by the navy, make a suicidal attempt to break out of Loch Riddon. While the larger ships engaged with the *Kingfisher* and her sisters, most of the smaller ships, he reasoned, would make good their escape. Not surprisingly, the crews of *Sophia*, *David* and *Anna* all objected, news of which was carried to the commander by Hume. To make matters worse, many of his Highlanders began to desert, adding to the earl's general sense of misery. In addition, the supply problem was now so serious that it was difficult even to feed those who remained. All that remained was a westward march across Cowal by the head of Loch Striven, and then across Loch Long into Dunbartonshire. Command of Eilean Dearg was given to Robert Elphinston, the same officer who refused to land at Greenock. He was left with fifty men and given orders to blow up the little castle and the remaining military stores if the Royal Navy should succeed in making a close approach. The prisoners from Orkney were also left in his care. With some difficulty, the seamen were persuaded to remain with the ships, which they were ordered to scuttle on the appearance of the enemy, and then take refuge with Elphinston in the castle. These dispositions having been made, the rest of the army moved off on their aimless march to the west. It was now 11 June; far to the south Monmouth was at last setting foot on English soil.

For three days after leaving the shores of Loch Riddon, Argyll stayed in Glendaruel, hoping to raise fresh Campbell recruits, ignoring his present supply problems. At this time the balance of influence in the army shifted decidedly against him. Only 500 Highlanders were left. The rest of the force, some 700 men, was made up of the Lowlanders and Kintyre volunteers. Having done so much to undermine the authority of the general, Hume decided on a change of tack, doing what he could to raise his morale, urging him ever onwards towards the Lowlands.[13] Loch Long was reached close to Ardentinny. A loyalist force commanded by Locheil was sent in pursuit, arriving too late to prevent the escape of the enemy. Using all the boats available, the rebels managed to complete the crossing to the eastern bank by night. No sooner was the lengthy crossing complete than they received news which helped throw Argyll back into a mood of despair: Eilean Dearg Castle had fallen.

Contrary to expectations, the Royal Navy managed to negotiate through the narrow waters of the Kyles of Bute. Coming under fire, Elphinston and his small garrison panicked and ran away, seeking cover in the woods of Portaneila, without attempting a defence.[14] Argyll's sailors also ran off, without scuttling the ships, which immediately fell into the hands of the navy. Before leaving Eilean Dearg, Elphinston made an attempt to blow up the stores by setting light to a trail of gunpowder. But amazingly, in his rush to get away, he left the Orkney prisoners behind, who immediately alerted Captain Hamilton. There was sufficient time to land a shore party, which extinguished the fuse and captured the military stores and all the rebel standards, later presented to the king. Hamilton subsequently reported that he had taken 400 barrels of powder, and sufficient arms for 3000 men. Among the stores were some new inventions, including 'a dagger to fly out beyond a muzzle', possibly the first mention of the bayonet in the British Isles, still a fairly new device at that time.[15] As soon as all the munitions were removed, the little castle was blown up, so completely that only a few stones remained.[16]

Bit by bit the net around the rebels began to tighten. At the head of the Gareloch they received word that the Duke of Gordon was advancing with a large body of men to join Atholl, and the Earl of Dumbarton had stationed many of his regular troops and militia at Glasgow, presumably on the assumption that Argyll's only remaining option was to attempt to break out to the south. A council of war was summoned to assess the position, at which the general declared his intention to engage the enemy at the first opportunity, in what appears to be a last desperate attempt to breath fresh life into an endeavour that was so obviously dying on its feet. True to form, Hume objected, saying that as much of the arms and ammunition was now lost, it was madness to think of fighting 'to lose the remaine of our hopes in one desperate attemp.'[17] Instead he suggested that the army, now little more than 900 men, should be divided in three. With one part of this army, his own Highlanders, Argyll would then return north to Glen Coe at the head of Loch Long, which, in Hume's estimation, could be held against 1000 men. Once firmly placed in Argyllshire, the earl might mount an effective guerrilla campaign, and thus attract more recruits to the cause. The remaining two parties, Lowlanders mostly, would then sail down Loch Long and the Gareloch, attempting to land where the enemy defences were weakest, and then sweep the countryside for sympathisers. Hume concluded by saying that instead of risking all on one last gamble, there would then be three chances of success.

It is difficult to know which proposal is the more suicidal, Hume's or Argyll's. In the circumstances, the earl was probably right in insisting that the small army be held together, for once overruling Hume, 'After much more discourse, the Earle remaind obstinately impersuadable, and as opinitive and wilful as ever: But said, any, that would not goe with him, might doe as they pleased; his intention was not to fight the enemie if he could shift them, but march straight to Glasgow, and there doe the next best.'[18]

It was now Tuesday 16 June. Along the shores of the Gareloch, the army marched in a southerly direction, having spent five weeks in the Highlands, neither able to do one thing or the other. That night the River Leven was crossed, just to the north of the great rock of

Dumbarton. The following morning they caught sight of the first royal troops, a body of horsemen on a nearby hilltop. Believing this was the advance guard of the whole government army, Argyll ordered his men to arms, taking up a well-protected position. After a time it became clear that the enemy force was only a small party of militia, unlikely to attempt any interference with the march of the larger rebel army. Rather than approach Glasgow by the direct route to the east, most likely guarded by strong enemy formations, Argyll ordered an advance north-east to Kilmarnock, close to the southern shores of Loch Lomond. After a short rest, the army continued with its weary trek, taking the road that leads from Dumbarton to Stirling. On the approach to Killearn, the scouts spotted more enemy troops, far stronger than before, but still isolated from the main army.

For Argyll, the opportunity he had sought for so long had now come. At last, on the frontier between the Highlands and Lowlands, it might be possible to engage the enemy with some prospect of success. In deciding to risk an attack, he was supported by Cochran and John Ayloff, who agreed that this opportunity could not be allowed to slip away. Although stronger, they had information that the loyalists were unprepared, as neither their commander nor their ammunition had as yet arrived. But the chance of a sudden and successful assault, slight as it may have been, was ruined by yet another debate in the council of war. Hume at once got to work: they were too weak, too dispirited, completely unfit to attempt an attack on government troops. He had, as Fountainhall remarks, 'an accumulation of reasons against everything that was proposed, being never satisfied with anything he met with'.[19] Instead he insisted on the onward march to Glasgow, now even more dangerous with enemy troops so close to their rear. For once he appears to have been in a minority, although possibly with more influence among the ordinary troops than Argyll. In the end, all came to nothing; for the time taken in debate had used up the advantage of surprise. The enemy was now aware of their presence and better organised than before. Rumbold tried to retrieve the situation by proposing a night attack, but this too was rejected. All that remained was to use the cover of night to attempt to slip away, thus avoiding close pursuit the following day. Even in the best of circumstances, night marches are difficult. For this army, continually beset by misfortune and indecision, it was to be an utter disaster.

9

Death and the Maiden

The earlier signs of intellectual paralysis that had gripped Argyll now returned, and were to remain for the rest of his forlorn adventure. With the enemy troops concentrating to his front, he was advised that a shift to a stronger position was necessary. Seemingly in a trance-like state, he sanctioned the change, giving no words of command beyond that. More like a rabble than an army, his troops moved to the new ground with their ranks broken and disordered. At this point they could hardly have escaped destruction if the enemy had advanced, but it was now too late in the day to risk an attack. As night fell, both sides set up camp close to Duntreath Castle. Morale in Argyll's camp, already weak, plummeted still further as the men were panicked by false rumours that their opponents were marching through the dark. For these tired and anxious men, there was to be no rest that night. No sooner had their fires been lit, than they were ordered to prepare for a march towards Glasgow, approximately twelve miles away from their present position.[1] This was dangerous, marshy country, full of risks for the unwary; but it would at least prevent an early pursuit, and Argyll had managed to secure the services of some local guides.

To deceive the enemy, fresh fuel was added to the campfires as the army marched off in silence. But the guides, probably more through incompetence than treachery, took them off in the wrong direction towards Kilpatrick, a small town on the River Clyde, ten miles to the west of Glasgow. Beset by fear, and shrouded in darkness, the rebels collapsed in confusion, one unit marching into another. Some were trapped in the bogs, others lost in the dark, and many simply ran away. Argyll from the rear tried to halt the march to bring the stragglers back together, and Rumbold was sent off to organise the leading formations. He, too, was lost in the dark. As day dawned on 18 June only 500 men remained, all exhausted by the ordeal. Having lost all hope, they soon began to scatter, making off in all directions. Some of the most determined, no more than 150 men, all that was left of the army, managed to force their way across the Clyde under fire from a militia company.[2]

At Kilpatrick, Argyll, clearly on the verge of mental collapse, and unsure whether to cross the Clyde or make his way back to the Highlands, sought the advice of Sir John Cochran. Cochran told him that his best course of action was to return to Argyllshire, hardly the most sensible advice, given the large number of government soldiers now between the earl and Inveraray. He left in the company of only four men – his son John, Sir Duncan Campbell, Major Fullarton and a Captain Duncanson.[3] No sooner had the small party set out than they decided that it was wiser to separate. Argyll also changed his mind. Sir Duncan Campbell and Captain Duncanson agreed to go on to Argyllshire in an attempt to raise more men, while Argyll with John and Fullerton decided to remain, hoping to take refuge in the nearby house of an old servant. Not surprisingly, the frightened man refused admission to the fugitives. With no option left, Argyll decided to follow Hume and Cochran into the Covenanter heartlands south of the Clyde. At some point he separated from John, who also went back to the north. Disguised as Fullarton's servant, Argyll attempted to cross the Clyde at the ford of Inchinnan. Here they were intercepted by some mounted militiamen. Fullarton tried to distract them while Argyll slipped away. He was spotted and fired on by two of the militiamen sent to intercept him. In the confused struggle that followed, a drunken weaver by the name of John Riddell, came out of a nearby cottage armed with a broadsword, the flat of which he used to strike the earl on the head, who promptly collapsed. He is said to have fallen with the words 'Ah! unfortunate Argyll', although this was almost certainly added later to give the story some more colour.[4] Riddell was later given a £50 reward for his services.

After crossing the Clyde, Hume and Cochran appear to have decided to attempt to link up with Monmouth, quite impossible in the circumstances. It would have been difficult enough to break out of Lowland Scotland, now dense with loyal troops, let alone advance all the way to south-west England. In fact they only managed to get as far as Muirdyke, near Lochwinnoch in Renfrewshire, where a large party of enemy soldiers halted their further progress.[5] Under the direction of Sir John Cochran, who was now to show himself as a soldier of courage and ability, the exhausted men were placed in a good defensive position. No sooner was one attack beaten off on the left than another followed on the right. The fighting was brief but fierce, coming to a hand-to-hand struggle with halberds. Unable to break the rebel resolve, the loyalists fell back for a second time. Other attacks followed with no more success, until the onset of night prevented any further fighting. Shrouded by the darkness, the rebels slipped away. They held together until news came that Argyll had been captured, thus marking an end to the organised phase of the rising. Clearly aware that the chances of reaching Monmouth were far from good, Cochran allowed the little force to disperse, each man looking to his own personal safety.

The skirmish at Muirdyke was to be the largest engagement of the whole Argyll Rising. Of little significance in itself, it demonstrates, perhaps, what might have been achieved if a greater strength of purpose had been shown from the outset. If seventy weary men could fight with such resolution, how much more could have been achieved by 2000 well-armed soldiers? Of course, it's impossible to answer this question in any convincing way, because many other factors could have intervened; all that can be said is that, in dealing with this emergency, Cochran had been allowed to act like a commander, free from the interference of armchair strategists, an opportunity that evaded Argyll throughout the campaign.

Far to the south, the same day as the capture of Argyll and the fight at Muirdyke, Monmouth entered the town of Taunton in Somerset. He was well received by the local people, many of whom were religious dissenters strong in their Whig sympathies. However, he had some serious worries: London and Cheshire showed no sign of rising and there was as yet no definite news of Argyll. Most serious of all, despite former promises of support, few of the local gentry rallied to the cause, leaving Monmouth, like some seventeenth-century Che Guevara, in command of an army largely made up of workers and peasants. To try and remedy the situation he took a fateful step, apparently on the advice of Ferguson and Lord Grey. Two days after the rebels entered Taunton a proclamation was read at the Market Cross.

> Whereas upon the decease of our Sovereign Lord King Charles the Second . . . the right of succession to the Crown . . . did legally descend and devolve upon the most illustrious and high-born Prince, James, Duke of Monmouth, son and heir-apparent of the said King Charles the Second; but James, Duke of York (taking advantage of the absence of the said James, Duke of Monmouth, beyond the seas) did first cause the said King to be poisoned and immediately thereon did usurp and invade the Crown and doth continue to do so. We, therefore, the noblemen, gentlemen and commoners here assembled . . . for the deliverance of the Kingdom from popery, tyranny and oppression, do recognise, publish and proclaim the said high and mighty Prince, James, Duke of Monmouth, our lawful and rightful sovereign and King, by the name of James the Second.[6]

Monmouth thus assumed a royal title, contrary to the promise he had made to Argyll and others. Even so it made little difference; the gentry still failed to appear. Faced with successive disappointments, Monmouth, always the reluctant rebel, began to demonstrate the weakness of a character that had only ever grown rich on flattery and easy success. As his army continued on its rather aimless progress through the West Country he sank steadily into a mood of despair, even considering at one point fleeing back to Holland. Faced with successive desertions, the news of Argyll's capture came as 'a very great balk to him and gave a sudden damp to his spirits.'[7]

As always he was prodded on by others, including Robert Ferguson, for whom the rising seems to have satisfied a lifetime of frustrated longing. At one point he was seen marching along the road brandishing a sword and shouting 'I am Ferguson! The famous Ferguson, for whose head so many hundreds of pounds were offered! I am that man! I am that man!' Under the influence of this single-minded fanatic, Monmouth marched on to his doom.

After his capture, Argyll was bound and escorted to the Earl of Dumbarton's headquarters in Glasgow by a party of militia, commanded by Sir John Shaw, the Laird of Greenock. Before being sent on to Edinburgh, he is said to have conversed with one Thomas Crawford, an old friend, saying 'Thomas, it hath pleased providence to frown on my attempt: but remember, I tell you, ere long one shall take up this quarrel whose shoes I am not worthy to bear, who will not miscarry in His undertaking.'[8] In this he was anticipating the arrival of William of Orange, who was to topple the crown from James' head not many years after the death of Argyll. However, this story is an obvious invention, first appearing the following century in Robert Wodrow's monumental treatise on the sufferings of the Scottish Church under the Stewarts. Nothing is known of Argyll's ability as a prophet; but as he never demonstrated any great reverence for the Dutch Stadholder, it seems wrong to cast him in the role of John the Baptist. William, always hedging his bets, had also tried to mollify James by responding quickly to his request, made at the height of the emergency, to send over the Scottish regiments in the Dutch service. These soldiers were in sight of St Abb's Head when they received word that Argyll had been taken, together with instructions that they should return to Holland.[9]

While Argyll was escorted to Edinburgh under heavy guard, the sweep continued for his fellow rebels. A reward was offered for the capture of Patrick Hume, previously denounced as a rebel for his part in the Rye House Plot. Evading the government patrols, he eventually escaped from Scotland to Ireland, and from thence to Utrecht by way of Bordeaux and Geneva, later becoming the first Earl of Marchmont during the reign of William of Orange. Sir Duncan Campbell of Auchinbreck also managed to get to Holland. Their comrades were not so lucky. Cochran was taken after his hideout was betrayed by the authorities, although he managed to escape execution, apparently after his father paid a large bribe. Richard Rumbold was caught near Lesmahagow, as he was trying to make for the border, being severely wounded in the process. John Ayloff, the other old soldier of the New Model Army, was also captured, attempting suicide by stabbing himself while imprisoned in Glasgow. He was later taken to London for execution. John Campbell was rounded up near Stirling, while his brother Charles was taken in his native Argyllshire, narrowly escaping summary execution by the timely intervention of the Marquis of Atholl. He was lucky, for as many as seventeen gentlemen of his clan, including Walter Campbell of Skipness, were hanged at *Rudha na H-Airde-rainich* – Bracken Point – where the town of Inveraray now stands.[10] One of them, Major Campbell, had his arms cut off prior to death. Many lesser individuals were also rounded up, including one William Campbell of Islay, who pleaded for mercy, claiming that he had been forced out after Rumbold threatened to kill him.[11] Jean Yeason, one of the Dutch soldiers, also attempted to save himself by claiming that he knew no more of Argyll's design 'then the child unborn'.

For the authorities, all that remained was to stamp out the embers of rebellion. Carnassarie Castle, the last centre of organised resistance in Argyllshire, was besieged by a party of Macleans under Kenneth Mackenzie of Suddie. It was only after some of the local gentry were rounded up and threatened with execution that the garrison agreed to surrender on terms. No sooner had the victors entered than one of the rebels, more determined than the rest, tried to blow the castle up, and thus kill both victors and vanquished in the process. He only succeeded in burning down part of the fortress. In a fury the Macleans attacked the prisoners, lynching Alexander Campbell, Auchinbreck's uncle, and wounding twenty others before they could be stopped.[12]

With Argyllshire now prostrate, the anti-Campbell clans got to work, plundering freely in a convenient loyalist guise, not bothering to inquire too deeply into the political allegiance of their victims. Even Breadalbane's Glengarry tenants were not exempt, causing him to write to Atholl in a mood of outrage: 'For Godsak secuir us from these base villanes befor you leav that shyr, from these murthering base villanes who never serv'd the King, and yet ther loyaltie must be cry'd up beyond my poor men who have left all they hav to their mercie for to serve the King. If the lyk of this be sufferable, judge of it, for I will not get a man to stay with me . . . I am very angry.'[13]

Although the ravaging of Clan Campbell was later to be known as the Atholl Raid, there appears to have been little the marquis could do to stop the anarchy unleashed in the wake of the rebellion. He at least gave orders that thieves and robbers masquerading as soldiers should be arrested. It has to be said, though, that he did not himself set a very good example, apparently stealing some trees from Argyll's estate. Besides, given that many of his men were, like the Macleans and Keppoch Macdonalds, ordinary clansmen with a grudge against the Campbells rather than professional soldiers, it was almost impossible to distinguish them from freelance bandits. For the rest of the summer robbery and casual violence were happening on a regular basis. It wasn't until September that things finally started to settle down, by which time the Campbells had been systematically stripped of just about anything of any value, later detailed in a comprehensive inventory.[14]

On Saturday 20 June Argyll entered Edinburgh, to be taken to the castle for the fourth and last time in his life. On the instructions of the Privy Council, which decided on public humiliation, he was led through the streets by the hangman, his head uncovered and his hands tied behind his back. Fountainhall notes his arrival and the transformation of his fortunes: 'Argile in pomp and glory carrid our imperiall croun before the King when Duke of York in his Parliament of 1681; and now, in 4 years' tyme, he is ignominiously led up that same street by the hangman.'[15]

Once in the castle, every precaution was taken to ensure that he would not escape a second time, which included putting him in irons. Rather than waste time on a new trial, it was decided that he should die under the manifestly unjust sentence of 1681. Ironically, this helped to ensure the speedy restoration of the house of Argyll after the Revolution of 1688: to reverse a sentence of forfeiture against a rebel and a traitor was one thing, and that on a man condemned for bad judgement quite another. James left the manner of Argyll's death to the Privy Council, although he gave implicit instructions that he should be tortured prior to his death to extract information about his associates:

'It is our will and pleasure to take all wayes to know from him those things which concern our government most, as his assisters with men, armes or money, his associates or correspondents, his designs etc.'[16]

This process, however, was not to delay his execution, which James instructed should be carried out within three days of the receipt of his letter, which arrived in Edinburgh on 29 June. Argyll was closely questioned, although he gave nothing of any substance away; there is no evidence that he was ever tortured. In accordance with James' wishes, the Council ordered that he be executed the following day. Prior to his death he did his best to plead for those who followed him, especially his son John, who on account of a disability to his hands was unable to bear arms, and had only come as a companion to his father. Although John and Charles were also sentenced to die, the sentence was later remitted to one of banishment. John's own son would one day help to defeat the Jacobites at Culloden, going on to become the fourth Duke of Argyll.

Although preoccupied with his own coming end, Argyll found time to express sympathy for the loyal Rumbold, who was executed in Edinburgh on 26 June – 'Poor Rumbold was a great support to me and a brave man and died Christianly.' Defiant to the last, the old warrior uttered a democratic clarion call from the scaffold: 'This is a deluded generation, veiled in ignorance, that though popery and slavery be riding in upon them, do not perceive it; though I am sure that there was no man born marked by God above another; for none comes into this world with a saddle on his back, neither any booted and spurred to ride him . . . '[17]

A twelve o'clock on Monday, 30 June, Argyll was handed over to the custody of the city magistrates, and taken under strong guard to the council chambers, where he was to remain until the time appointed for his execution. Just over two hours later he was beheaded by the Maiden, the same device that had been used to execute his father, dying with calmness and courage. Prior to this he penned his own epitaph in verse.

> Thou Passenger, that shalt have so much time
> To view my grave, and ask what was my crime,
> No stain of error, no black vices brand, was that
> which chas'd me from my native land.
> Love to my country – twice sentenced to die –
> Constraint my hands forgotten arms to try.
> More by friends' fraud my fall proceeded hath
> Than foes, tho' now they thrice decreed my death.
> Of my attempt, tho' providence did frown,
> His oppress'd people God at length shall own.
> Another hand, by more successful speed,
> Shall raise the remnant, bruise the serpent's head.
> Tho' my head fall, that is no tragick story,
> Since going hence, I enter endless glory.[18]

Argyll's refusal to be reconciled with the present regime continued even after he mounted the scaffold, where he gave a speech that concluded with a clear reference to James.

It is suggested to me that I have said nothing of the royall familie and it remembers me, that befor the justice at my tryall about the Test, I said that at my death I wold pray that ther should never want one of the royall familie to be a defender of the trew, ancient, apostolicall, catholicall Protestant faith, which noe I doe, and that God wold enlighten and forgive all of them that are lukewarme or have shrunk from the profession of it, and in all events I pray God may provide for the security of his church against Antichrist nor the gates of hell may prevail against it.[19]

That same day his young grandson fell out of a three-storey window and survived, which was interpreted as a sign that the house of Argyll would one day recover from the power of its enemies. He grew up to be one of the greatest statesmen and soldiers ever produced by the Campbells – Red John of the Battles, the second Duke of Argyll. When in later life he was challenged by his aunt for opposing James' son in the Jacobite Rising of 1715 he responded by saying 'That family, madam, oues me and my family two heads, whereof your father was one; and it becomes you ill to propose this question.'[20] However, the fall of a second Campbell head in a generation was pleasing to Iain Lom.

But it would please me to see the Campbells snarling
Together under the ridge-pole of the French Tower and a
Very tight fetter on their sinews.

The dark-grey chastening Maiden left the Earl without
Longevity, and took the choler out of the Marquis of
Argyll . . .[21]

Monmouth fared no better than Argyll in his own endeavours. Now alone and virtually trapped in the south-west, his army was intercepted and defeated on 6 July at the Battle of Sedgemoor in Somerset, in what was to be the last pitched battle ever fought on English soil. A few days after this Monmouth was captured and taken to London, where he was executed on 15 July. A pathetic and tragic figure, he showed little of the resolve of Rumbold or Argyll, spending his last days pleading in desperation for his life. Argyll's death was merciful compared with that of Monmouth. After five strokes of the axe his head had still not come off, and finally had to be removed with a knife. The crowd was so angry that Jack Ketch, the incompetent executioner, had to be escorted away by a party of soldiers in fear of his life.

Robert Ferguson, who had done as much as anyone to bring King Monmouth to his wretched fate, managed to escape back to Holland. He later accompanied William of Orange on his voyage to England in 1688, although the Dutchman, with better sense than Monmouth, paid him little heed. With an almost unbelievable lack of consistency, and in a fury of frustrated ambition, the Plotter, who had spent so much of his life trying to remove the Stewarts from the throne, later became a Jacobite. In his *History of the Revolution*, published in 1706, he made the astonishing claim that William's voyage to England 'was a deep and successful design of the Vatican for the advancement of popery throughout the whole of Europe.'[22] Urged on by the restless demon that governed his nature, he was involved in plot after plot, finally dying in poverty in 1714.

The reasons for the failure of the Argyll Rising are not hard to find: there were no clear objectives, either military or political, and the leadership was catastrophically divided. There is, however, something more: the character of Argyll himself. Gilbert Burnet, although generally sympathetic to the cause, highlights the arrogance of the Campbell chief, which led him to underestimate the difficulties he was likely to encounter in Scotland. More than this, at the height of his power, he had acted more as a landlord – and not a particularly sympathetic one at that – rather than a clan chief in the traditional sense. Hence his people, contrary to the exaggerated hopes he had entertained in Amsterdam, failed to appear when his need was greatest. Burnet understood this very well: 'He had not behaved himself in his prosperity like a man that thought he might at some time or another need the affections of his people . . . for though he always reckoned that he was sure he could raise 5000 men in his country yet he could not bring together five and twenty hundred men to come to him.'[23]

Although the risings of Argyll and Monmouth had failed, they had the paradoxical effect of hurrying James to his ruin. He saw his triumph as a sign that God approved his regime and wished him to advance the Catholic cause.[24] Believing himself to be unassailable, and lacking the intelligence, good sense and political skill of his brother, he gradually alienated virtually the whole of the English political establishment, both Whig and Tory. The last straw was the birth of his son James in June 1688, which opened the prospect of a permanent Catholic dynasty. His enemies united to invite William and Mary to take his place. Archibald, Lord Lorne, who had gone into exile some time before, accompanied William to England. In 1689, now the tenth Earl of Argyll, he came to London to offer the crown of Scotland jointly to William and Mary, providing his father with a little posthumous earthly glory.

Epilogue

James was said to have been so angered by Argyll's rebellion that for a time he even considered abolishing the very name of Campbell, in much the same way that his grandfather James VI had proscribed the name of Macgregor. He was only prevented from doing so by the loyalty of the Earl of Breadalbane. One thing was certain: the eclipse of the house of Argyll was complete. In the early 1660s the many enemies of the Campbells, encouraged by the execution of the Marquis of Argyll, had been frustrated in their attempts to destroy his son. Lord Lorne may have been the son of a traitor, but he himself had a clear record of loyalty to the crown, confirmed by his role in the Glencairn Rising. His son, in contrast, had no such record, and was defined solely by his descent from two generations of traitors. Even Lorne's conversion to Catholicism, a move that usually worked with James, failed to have any effect. Lorne soon left for the continent, all thoughts of Catholicism forgotten, to plan other ways of restoring his family's fortunes.

James, meantime, was left with a problem: how was the vacuum left by the departure of the Campbells to be filled? He had an opportunity, it might be thought, to remodel an ancient power structure in the Highlands, to build upon the perceived loyalty of the anti-Campbell clans. Never the most imaginative of men, however, he was soon seeking old solutions to new problems. Yet there had been a revolutionary transformation of Highland politics, quite beyond anything any previous Stewart monarch could have conceived.

For hundreds of years, the clans of the Highlands and Islands had been deeply hostile to the interference of alien Lowland governments in their affairs, seeking always to maintain their own independence. When lawless chiefs were summoned to Edinburgh they often simply hid away among their kin, defying the best efforts of the state to bring them to justice. There was little tradition of loyalty towards the Stewarts or even towards Scotland itself. Before the Union of the Crowns, many chiefs were quite prepared to enter into treasonable associations with the English. In 1545, for example, thousands of Highlanders and Islanders gathered under the banner of Donald Dubh Macdonald, the last serious claimant to the Lordship of the Isles, who entered into an alliance with Henry VIII to make war on the Scottish crown. Highlanders, moreover, were often engaged in murderous internal feuds, completely ignoring the efforts of the king to maintain a semblance of law and order. A mere hundred years before the rebellion of 1685, a feud between the Macleans of Duart and the Macdonalds of Dunyveg erupted into a full-scale war, embracing virtually all of the Western Isles and drawing in Spanish and English mercenaries – an intolerable situation for any sovereign state.

For James VI (of Scotland, I of England) the suggestion that the wild western clans could be loyal to the crown would have been quite preposterous. He once described the people of the Isles as 'utterly barbarous', and had gone so far as to approve a Lowland attempt to colonise Lewis, which was to be based on the wholesale extermination of the local people. At the dawn of the seventeenth century, the outlawed Macgregors were being hunted and executed with a thoroughness probably inconceivable in any other part of mainland Britain. After 1603, James, safe on his throne in London, would be pleased to have his prejudices against the clansmen confirmed by William Shakespeare, whose play *Macbeth*, written in about 1610, contains the following lines:

> The merciless Macdonwald,
> Worthy to be a rebel, for to that
> The multiplying villanies of nature
> Do swarm upon him, from the Western Isles
> Of kerns and galloglasses is supplied.[1]

It was against this background that the Macdonalds of Dunyveg fell to destruction, losing their lands on Kintyre to the seventh Earl of Argyll, and those on Islay to Campbell of Cawdor. In the wild west, the Campbells, as far back as the fourteenth century, had been the law-men, a role shared in the east by the Gordons of Huntly and further north by the Mackenzies of Kintail. But it was the Campbells, skilful practitioners of feudal law, who often incurred the greatest resentment.

It was once argued that the feudal system, by placing too much power in the hands of families like the Campbells, distorted the 'natural' relationship between the clans and the crown.[2] In other words, once free from their feudal tutelage, the Highlanders, living in conservative and kin-based societies, would give their support to the legitimate ruling house. But there is virtually no evidence to support this before the outbreak of the Civil Wars, and even then the loyalty that began to emerge was highly dependent on local circumstances. Even before the Civil Wars the Highlands had been changing, especially after the Union of the Crowns and the establishment of the Lowland Plantation in Ulster began to weaken the old links between the Gaelic peoples of Ireland and Scotland. The large-scale independent warfare, of the type that had been fought out in the previous century between the Macleans and Macdonalds, was now clearly a thing of the past. However, there was little to show that the Highlanders had any real enthusiasm for the king, who, far away in London, was an even more remote figure than he had been in the past. As late as 1624, the leader of the Macdonalds of Clanranald, a wholehearted convert to Catholicism, wrote to the Pope effectively proposing a crusade against the Protestant crown.[3]

The split between the Campbells and the king in the 1630s opened up, as we have seen, an entirely new prospect. Throughout the Highlands and Islands there was a dramatic change in the patterns of loyalty and rebellion. Outsiders became insiders, regardless of their religion. Nevertheless, for the Highlanders, the Civil War was a struggle *against* the Campbells rather than *for* the king; the career of the great Alasdair MacColla provides a perfect example of this. His struggle had clear limits, and he cannot really be seen as a forerunner of the later Jacobites; it was simple hatred of the Campbells that provided the chief motivation for Alasdair and his fellow Gaels. It might be argued that the later Glencairn Rising, aside from the abysmal leadership, never really took off because it was deprived of this focus by the royalism of

Lord Lorne. The nascent alliance between the clans and the crown, if not completely broken, was rendered obsolete by Lorne's restoration in 1663. It re-emerged in 1689, but under circumstances quite different from the past.

James, both as Duke of York and as king, was one of the few Stewarts to express any real sympathy for the Highland clans who had given so much for his family; but only insofar as they could be of use to him, setting the scene for his grandson, Charles Edward Stewart, who later urged the Highlanders to carry him to London, regardless of the cost. There is absolutely no evidence to suggest that James ever considered a revolutionary change in the feudal structure of the Highlands. His attack on Argyll in 1681 was almost certainly based on an attempt to reduce rather than eliminate the power of the Campbells. It was the precipitate flight of the earl that forced a change in emphasis; but only, it has to be stressed, on the margins. The feudal superiorities that had belonged to Argyll were redistributed, not eliminated. In other words, the same patters of domination and dependence, such a source of resentment in the Highlands, continued much as before, a change of name taking the place of a change in policy. Cameron of Locheil, for example, once a vassal of Argyll, became a vassal of the Duke of Gordon. James was later to reverse this decision, giving Locheil the personal independence he had always desired. However, and again this has to be stressed, Locheil was not treated as a 'natural' chief with authority solely over his own kin. Rather he was promised his own little feudal empire, which was to include Sunart and Ardnamurchan, areas formerly controlled by the Campbells, although this was not Cameron country.

James' treatment of Locheil seems to have been largely based on personal friendship, which allowed the Highlander an almost unique access to the royal court. It was never more than a special case, although James was later to claim from the hindsight of exile that he intended to treat other chiefs in a similar fashion. No doubt once safely back in London, and subject to other pressures and considerations, he would have changed his mind. His one-sided treatment of Locheil had a paradoxical effect. In the short run it did much to ensure that James' short reign was one of the most unstable in Highland history; in the long run it helped give the final shape to the Jacobite movement, further galvanised by a fear of a Campbell resurrection.

In general, the disappearance of the Campbells brought little peace to the Highlands. If anything, the problems became more intense. In March 1686, the newly created Commission for Pacifying the Highlands wrote to General Drummond, pleading for more troops, and indicating just how far they had failed in their mission: 'The reason quherof is that the thieves of Glencoan and Lochaber have not only already fallen upon the neighbouring places . . . but these thieves come down in tens and tuelves to the braes of Strathern and the Ochzells in armes thigging, and if they be denyed there they steall and robbe, so that the gentlemen in these countries have not safety nor securitie to themselves.'[4]

In September of that same year, Drummond was forced to march in person into Argyllshire, where broken rebels and thieves appear to have made a common cause, no doubt encouraged by the power vacuum. No sooner was a problem solved in one location, than a new one promptly appeared in another. By the summer of 1688, the last of James' reign, thieving and depredation were reaching epic proportions. To make matters worse, Coll Macdonald of Keppoch, perhaps encouraged by James' one-sided treatment of Locheil, recently freed from vassalage to the Duke of Gordon, rose in arms to defend his territorial rights against Lachlan Mackintosh of Clan Chatton, his own feudal superior. At Mulroy in August 1688, Mackintosh was defeated by a combined force of Camerons and Macdonalds, in what has sometimes been described as the last private clan battle. For the government, the real significance of the encounter was that Mackintosh had an official commission to remove Coll from Lochaber, and in that he was assisted by a troop of regular soldiers; moreover their commander, Kenneth Mackenzie of Suddie, who had served against Argyll in 1685, was killed in the action. Coll was duly outlawed, but continued to defy Mackintosh, James and the Privy Council. This notwithstanding, he was one of the first to declare for James after the Revolution, and enjoys the unique distinction of being in rebellion against two kings at the same time.

James could, perhaps, have made his own position in the Highlands more secure by extending the treatment of Locheil to other chiefs, like Coll of Keppoch. Nevertheless, any advantage he gained by this is likely to have been more than offset by the resentment of powerful vested interests. Argyll was gone, but the Marquis of Atholl, the Duke of Gordon and the Earl of Breadalbane were no less jealous of their own hereditary rights, as were lesser men like Lachlan Mackintosh. Put another way, James might have secured the loyalty of the clan chiefs, but only by alienating the men he relied upon to govern the Highlands.

Some of the clans, it has to be said, like the Camerons and Macdonalds, were bound to fight for James,

regardless of the circumstances. They knew little of
William of Orange, except that he carried in his wake
the promised resurrection of a Lowland Presbyterian and
Whig establishment, bitterly resented in the Highlands.
Worst of all, he arrived in England in the company of
Lord Lorne, soon to be the tenth Earl of Argyll. For
Cameron of Locheil, so recently freed from Gordon, the
return of the old master was a particular threat. More
than any other, he galvanised the anti-Campbell clans in
Lochaber, who united behind the banner of John Graham
of Claverhouse, now Viscount Dundee. In this the
Jacobite movement was born, and the alliance between
the clans and the Stewarts, forged in the Civil Wars, was
finally recreated, more completely than before. Although
the Jacobite army enjoyed an early success at the Battle
of Killiecrankie, this was more than offset by the death
of Dundee. Later, under the uninspiring leadership of
Alexander Cannon, the clans were defeated at Dunkeld
by the Cameronian Regiment, commanded by William
Cleland, Argyll's old ally.

For the Campbells, the Revolution ended a long
interlude, recreating the axis between the clan and the
crown, broken during the reign of Charles I. As long as
the clan system continued to exist their power remained
unchallenged. They were the one great constant on the
Whig horizon, from the time of William and Mary
through to the Hanoverian Succession. In the end,
however, they were no more immune than their neighbours to the external forces that became increasingly
important as the years passed, being drawn ever deeper
into a Lowland money economy. Even before the last
Jacobite Rebellion, the second Duke of Argyll, ever more
attentive to the need to maximise his income, signalled
the death of the whole clan system by insisting that farms

on his estates be let to the highest bidders, rather than men bearing his own name.

The Jacobite movement of 1689 was born chiefly as part of an anti-Campbell reaction, thus emerging from the same womb as their Civil War predecessors. There was, however, one great difference. After 1689, it was no longer enough to defeat the Campbells; the real sources of enemy power lay far beyond the Highland line. In defending the rights of James and his descendants, the clansmen were inevitably drawn into a hopeless struggle on a national stage, with disastrous consequences for their way of life. Although the Jacobites, with a wider base of support, initially achieved a far greater success in 1689, 1715 and 1745 than Argyll in 1685, the end result was just the same. Paradoxically, it was the friendship of the Stewarts rather than the enmity of the Campbells that took the ancient warrior clans across the threshold of destruction. The old feudal superiorities were an anachronism and would eventually have disappeared, regardless of the outcome of the contest. Their abolition in the wake of the Battle of Culloden served as little more than advance warning that an old world was coming rapidly to an end.

Notes

FOREWORD

1. *Journal of John Erskine of Carnock* (ed.) W. Macleod, 1893, p.113.
2. Register of the Privy Council of Scotland, vol. XI, p.306 (hereinafter RPCS).
3. A collection of letters . . . to Sancroft, Archbishop of Canterbury. Perth to Sancroft, 1 July 1685.

CHAPTER 1

1. For the general background on Campbell–Macdonald relations at this time see Paterson, R. C, 2001.
2. See Paterson, R. C., 1998.
3. Hamilton Papers vol. 1, 1880 pp.12–13; Historical Manuscripts Commission Supplementary Report. Duke of Hamilton XXI, 1932, p.50.
4. Knowler, W. (ed.) vol II, 1841–2, p.187.
5. Robert Baillie vol. II, 1841–2, p.74.

6. Patrick Gordon of Ruthven, 1844, p.27.
7. Forbes-Leith, W. *Memoirs of Scottish Catholics,* 1909, pp.366–7.
8. Orian Iain Luim. *Songs of John MacDonald, Bard of Keppoch* (ed.) A. M. Mackenzie, 1964, pp.20–5.
9. Watson, W. J. *Scottish Verse from the Dean of Lismore* vol. II, 1937, p.75.
10. Paterson, R. C., 1998, p.174.
11. Firth, C. H. (ed.) *Scotland and the Commonwealth,* 1895, p. xlvii.
12. *The Case of the Earl of Argyll,* 1683, p.61.
13. *The Life of Edward, Earl of Clarendon* vol. II, 1857, p.39.
14. Firth, C. H., op. cit., pp.165–9.
15. Ibid., pp.166–7.
16. Robert Baillie, op. cit., vol. III, pp.250, 288.

CHAPTER 2

1. Robert Baillie, op. cit., vol. III, p.447.
2. Ibid., p.404.
3. Gilbert Burnet, 1823, vol. I, p.211.
4. George Mackenzie, 1821, p.39.
5. Hutton, R., 1989, p.172.
6. Orian Iain Luim, op cit., pp.79, 81.
7. Historical Manuscripts Commission 6th Report, 1877, p.621.
8. Kirkton, James, 1992 p.97; also Robert Wodrow vol. I, p.297.
9. *Diaries of the Lairds of Brodie,* 1863, p.218.
10. *Letters to the Argyll Family,* 1839, p.177.
11. *Correspondence of the Earl of Ancrum and the Earl of Lothian* vol. II, 1874, p.44.
12. *Diaries of the Lairds of Brodie,* op. cit., p.247.

13. George Mackenzie, op. cit., pp.70–1.
14. Gilbert Burnet, op. cit., p.252; John Nicoll p.369.
15. Ibid., p.373.
16. *Diaries of the Lairds of Brodie*, op. cit., p.267.
17. Gilbert Burnet, op. cit., pp.252–3.
18. Acts of the Parliament of Scotland vol. VIII, 1820, p.92.
19. George Mackenzie, op. cit., p.133; Gilbert Burnet, op. cit., pp.252–3.
20. George Mackenzie, op. cit., p.84.
21. John Lamont, 1830, p.162; John Nicoll, op. cit., p.394.
22. *Records of Argyll*, 1885 pp.21–5.
23. *Letters from Archibald to John, Earl of Argyll, Duke of Lauderdale*, 1829, pp.62–3.
24. Ibid., p.14.
25. Gilbert Burnet, op. cit., p.407.
26. *Letters from Archibald* etc., op. cit., pp.83–4.
27. McKerral A., 1948, p.42.
28. Lauderdale Papers vol. I, p.222; McKerral A., op. cit., p.119.
29. George Mackenzie, op. cit., p.177.
30. Hopkins, P. 1986, p.41.
31. Brodie diaries, op. cit., p.369; *Argyll's Declaration* 1685.
32. Papers relating to the Macleans of Duart, 1670–1680 in *Highland Papers* vol. I, 1914, p.246; Stevenson, D. 1980, p.280.
33. Orian Iain Luim, op cit., p.143.
34. Robert Law 1819, p.83.
35. Sir John Lauder of Fountainhall, *Historical Notices* etc., vol. I, 1848, p.108.
36. Brodie diaries, op. cit., p.391.

CHAPTER 3

1. Paterson, R. C., 1998, p.250.

2. Elder, J. R., 1914, see appendix.
3. Macinnes, A. I., 1986, p.187.
4. Kenyon, J., 1974, p.3.
5. Trevor, M., 1988, p.66.
6. Hopkirk, M., 1953, pp.44–5.
7. Fox, C. J., 1808, p.165.
8. RPCS vol. VI, 1914, (ed.) P. Hume Brown pp.165,170.
9. Paterson, R. C., 1998, p.253.
10. RPCS vol. VI, op. cit., p.222; R. Wodrow op. cit., vol. III p.84; Historical Manuscripts Commission 6th Report op. cit., p.622.
11. Lauderdale Papers, op. cit., vol. III, p.179.
12. Hopkins, P., op. cit., p.68.
13. Stevenson, D., op. cit., p.288.
14. Ibid. p.289.

CHAPTER 4

1. Hutton, R., op. cit, p.390.
2. Fountainhall, Historical Notices, op. cit., vol. I, p. 327.
3. Lang, A., 1909, p.217.
4. Willcock, J., 1907, p.249.
5. *The Case of the Earl of Argyll* op. cit., p.1.
6. Ibid., p.4; Willcock J., op. cit., pp.251–2.
7. Sir John Dalrymple vol. I, 1771 p.6.
8. *The Case of the Earl of Argyll*, op. cit., p.6.
9. RPCS vol. VII, (ed.) P. Hume Brown 1915, p.242.
10. Lang, A., op. cit., p. 223.
11. RPCS vol. VII, op. cit., p.244.
12. Ibid., pp.259–60.
13. Sir John Dalrymple, op. cit., vol. II, p.67.
14. Wodrow, R., op. cit., vol. III, p.76.
15. Fountainhall, Chronological Notices of Scottish Affairs, 1822, p.21.

16. Gilbert Burnet, op. cit,. p.352.
17. Fountainhall, *Historical Observes*, 1840, p.54.
18. James Macpherson vol. I, 1775 p.123; Sir John Dalrymple, op. cit p.8.
19. Gilbert Burnet, op. cit., p.312.
20. Willcock, J., op. cit., p.279.
21. RPCS 1915, p.91.
22. *Fountainhall, Historical Observes*, op. cit., pp.55–6; *An Account of the Arraignment, Tryal, Escape and Condemnation of a Dog* etc., 1682.

CHAPTER 5

1. Trench, C. C., 1969, p.36.
2. Ferguson, J., 1807.
3. *Dictionary of National Biography* vol. XVIII, 1889.
4. Trench, C. C., op. cit., p.116.
5. Ibid.
6. *Correspondence of the Family of Hatton* (ed.) E. M. Thompson, vol. II, p.296.
7. Willcock, J., op. cit., p.296.
8. *Calendar of State Papers Domestic*, Jan–Dec. 1682 (ed.) F. H. Blackburne Daniel 1932, p.170; *Memoirs of Veitch and Bryson* (ed.) T. McCrie 1825, p.142.
9. Macaulay, T. B., 1985, pp.409–10.
10. Greave, R. C., 1992, p.102.
11. Ford, Lord Grey, 1754, pp.22–3. *A letter giving a short and true account of the Earl of Argyll's invasion in the year 1685*; Halley, K. H. D., 1968, pp.710–11. Halley describes Argyll as a 'stiff Presbyterian', which he most assuredly was not.
12. *Memoirs of Veitch and Bryson*, op. cit., pp.142–4.
13. Willcock, J., op. cit., p.304; Hopkins, P., op. cit., p.96.

14. Sir John Dalrymple, op. cit., p.22.
15. Trench, C. C., p. cit., p.47.
16. Veitch and Bryson, op. cit., p.145; Robert Law, op. cit., p.236.
17. *Historical Manuscripts Commission 7*, op. cit., p.633.
18. *State Papers* etc. *to William Carstares* (Carstares State Papers) 1774, p.10.
19. Ibid., p.14.
20. James Macpherson, op. cit., p.323.

CHAPTER 6

1. Trench, C.C., op. cit., p.71.
2. RPCS vol. VIII, pp.509–11.
3. *Orian Iain Luim*, op. cit., pp.173, 175.
4. *Chronicles of the Atholl and Tullibardine Families* (hereinafter *Atholl Chronicles*) vol. I, 1908, pp.187, 188, 190, 192–3, 196.
5. Ibid., p.191.
6. Fountainhall, *Observes*, op. cit., p.142.
7. Trench, C. C., op. cit., p.73.
8. Bevan, B., 1973, p.186.
9. Sir John Dalrymple, op. cit., p.54.
10. Ford, Lord Grey, op. cit., p.109.
11. Fountainhall, *Observes*, op. cit., p.165.
12. Ibid., pp.166–7.
13. Ferguson, J., op. cit., p.196.
14. Patrick Hume, 1831, p.13.
15. Ibid., p.21.
16. Ibid., p.27.
17. Ibid., p.22.
18. Macaulay, T. B., op. cit., p.425.
19. Macaulay, T. B., op. cit., p.415.

20. Ibid., p.416; Carstares State Papers, op. cit., p.35n; Willcock, J., op. cit., p.348.

21. Ford, Lord Grey, op. cit., p.119.

22. Fountainhall, *Historical Notices*, op. cit., vol. II, pp.336–7.

23. Greaves, R. C., op. cit., pp.281–2.

24. Lingard, J., vol. X, 1883, p.151–1.

CHAPTER 7

1. *Calendar State Papers Domestic, James II*, 1960, p.127.

2. *Acts of the Parliament of Scotland*, op. cit., p.456.

3. Patrick Hume, op. cit., p.39.

4. *Diary of Thomas Brown, 1675–1693*, 1898 p.34–5; Patrick Hume, op. cit., p. 39; *Journal of John Erskine of Carnock*, op. cit., p.115.

5. Fox, C. J., op. cit., p.192.

6. *Journal of John Erskine of Carnock*, op. cit., p. 115; Patrick Hume, op. cit., p.167.

7. Fountainhall, *Observes*, op. cit., p.167.

8. *A letter* etc., op. cit., p.10; R. Wodrow, op cit., vol. IV pp.288–9.

9. Stevenson, D., p.292 and many others.

10. Hopkins, P., op., cit., p.96.

11. *Atholl Chronicles*, op. cit., p.201.

12. *Memoirs of Locheil* 1842, p.210.

13. *Atholl Chronicles*, op. cit., p.219.

14. Patrick Hume, op. cit., p.41; John Erskine op. cit., p.117.

15. *Argyll's Declaration* 1685, p.2.

16. John Erskine, op. cit., p.119; RPCS vol. X, (ed.) H. Paton 1927, p.307 onwards details individual cases.

17. Willcock, J., op. cit., Appendix II pp.433–4.

18. Mackenzie, W. C., 1935, p.27.

19. John Erskine, op. cit., pp.119–20.
20. Willcock, J., op. cit., p.368.
21. Wodrow, R., op. cit., p.298.

CHAPTER 8

1. Breadalbane Correspondence, Scottish Record Office GD 137/16; GD 137/18.
2. *Atholl Chronicles*, op cit., p.122.
3. John Erskine, op. cit., p.122; Reid J. E., 1864, p.95n.
4. Patrick Hume, op. cit., p.47; John Erskine op. cit., p.123.
5. Willcock J., op. cit., p.377; Macaulay, T.B., op cit., p.420.
6. R. Wodrow, op. cit., vol. IV p.293; Fountainhall, *Observes*, op. cit., p.168.
7. Patrick Hume, op. cit., p.49.
8. Ibid., p. 50.
9. Fountainhall, *Observes* op. cit., p.168.
10. *Atholl Chronicles*, op. cit., p.231.
11. Ibid., p.232.
12. Ibid., p.233; *Memoirs of Locheil*, op. cit., p.213; Fountainhall, *Observes*, op. cit., p.177.
13. Patrick Hume, op. cit., p.54.
14. *Atholl Chronicles*, op. cit., p.239; *Veitch and Bryson*, op. cit., p.315; Brown, A., 1889, p.401.
15. *Calendar of State Papers Domestic,* James II, p.206.
16. Eilean Dearg – Red Island – was long known locally, from the presence of a lonely tree, as One Tree Island. Like the castle, this has now gone. The site was excavated in the mid-1960s, when a large number of musket balls together with a Dutch navigational divide were discovered. See Argyll–An Inventory of Ancient Monuments, vol. 7, 1992, pp.282–3.
17. Patrick Hume, op. cit., p.55.

18. Ibid., p.56.
19. Fountainhall, *Observes*, op. cit., p.179.

CHAPTER 9

1. Patrick Hume, op. cit., p.61.
2. Ibid., pp.61–2; *Veitch and Bryson*, op. cit., pp.321–2.
3. Probably Robert Duncanson, a lifelong follower of the Argyll family. In 1692, as a major in the Argyll Regiment, he issued the order to Captain Robert Campbell of Glenlyon to begin the massacre of Glencoe.
4. Fountainhall, *Observes*, op. cit., p.181.
5. Patrick Hume, op. cit., pp.63–4; *Veitch and Bryson*, op. cit., pp.324–6.
6. Trench, C. C., op. cit., p.154.
7. Ibid., p.181.
8. R. Wodrow, op. cit., vol. IV, p.299.
9. Fountainhall, *Observes*, op. cit., p.176.
10. RPCS vol. VIII, op. cit., p.308.
11. *Atholl Chronicles* vol. V, 1908, p.clxxi; *Records of Argyll* op. cit., p.49.
12. *New Statistical Account of Scotland* vol. VII, 1845, p.557; *Atholl Chronicles* vol. I, op. cit., p. 254.
13. Ibid., p.256.
14. *An Account of the Depredations Committed upon Clan Campbell* etc. (ed.) A. Kincaid, 1816.
15. Fountainhall, *Observes*, op. cit., p.187.
16. RPCS vol. XI, (ed.) H. Paton 1929, pp.84–5.
17. *A Complete Collection of State Trials* vol. XI, 1816, p.882.
18. *The Argyle Papers* 1834, p.36.
19. Willcock, J., op. cit., p.379.
20. R. Wodrow, *Analecta* vol. II, 1842 p.308.

21. *Orian Iain Luim,* op cit., p.181.
22. *Dictionary of National Biography* vol. XVIII, 1889, p.352.
23. *English Historical Documents* vol. VIII, p.628.
24. Miller, J., 1977, p. 142.

EPILOGUE

1. *Macbeth* Act I, Scene II, lines 10–14.
2. Cunningham, A., *The Loyal Clans.*
3. Campbell, J. L.(ed.) the letter sent by John Muidertach etc, in the *Innes Review* vol. IV, 1953, pp.110–6.
4. RPCS vol. XII, (ed.) H. Paton, 1930, pp.2–3 .

Select bibliography

DOCUMENTARY AND NARRATIVE SOURCES

An Account of the Arraignment, Tryal, Escape and Condemnation of a Dog etc. 1682

Acts of the Parliament of Scotland, vols. VII, VIII, 1820, 1822

Argyll's Declaration, 1685

The Argyle Papers, 1834

Baillie, Robert, *Letters and Journals*, vol. III, 1862

Breadalbane Correspondence, Scottish Record Office

Brodie, Diaries of the Lairds of, 1863

Burnet, Gilbert, *History of His Own Time*, 1823

Browning, A., ed., *English Historical Documents*, vol. VIII 1953

Campbell, J. L. ed., 'The Letter sent by John Muidertach, twelfth Chief of Clanranald, to Pope Urban VIII', in the *Innes Review* vol. IV, pp. 110–6, 1953

Carstares, William, *State Papers*, 1774

The Case of the Earl of Argyle, 1683

Calendar of State Papers, of the Reign of Charles II, Domestic Series, variously edited, 1860–1939

Calendar of State Papers, of the Reign of James II, Domestic Series, 1960

Clarendon, Edward Earl of, *The Life of Edward Earl of Clarendon,* vol. II, 1857

Correspondence of the Earl of Ancrum and the Earl of Lothian, vol. II, 1874

Chronicles of the Atholl And Tullibardine Families, arranged by John Murray, 7th Duke of Atholl, vols I, V, 1908

A Complete Collection of State Trials, compiled by T. B. Howell, vol. VIII, 1816

Dalrymple, Sir John, *Memoirs of Great Britain and Ireland,* 1771

Drummond, John of Balhaldy, *Memoirs* 1842

Erskine, John, *Journal,* 1893

Firth, C. H., ed. *Scotland and the Commonwealth,* 1895

——, *Scotland and the Protectorate,* 1899

Forbes-Leith, W. *Memoirs of Scottish Catholics,* 1848

Ford, Lord Grey, *The Secret History of the Rye House Plot and the Monmouth Rebellion,* 1754

Fountainhall, Sir John Lauder of, *Chronological Notes of Scottish Affairs,* 1822

——, *Historical Observes,* 1840

——, *Historical Notices of Scottish Affairs,* 2 vols., 1848

Foxcroft, H. C., ed., *A Supplement to Burnet's History,* 1902

Historical Manuscripts Commission, Reports, 1877

Hume, Sir Patrick, *Narrative of the Earl of Argyle's Expedition,* Marchmont Papers, vol. III, 1831

Kincaid, A., ed., *An Account of the Depredations committed upon Clan Campbell and their followers etc.,* 1816

Kirkton, James, *A History of the Church of Scotland, 1660–1679,* 1992

Lamont, John, *Diary, 1649–1671,* 1830

Law, Robert, *Memorialls,* 1819

Letters from Archibald, Earl of Argyll to John, Duke of Lauderdale, 1829

Letters to the Argyll Family, 1839

A Letter Giving a short and true Account of the Earl of Argyls Invasion in the year 1685, 1686

Mackenzie, Sir George, of Rosehaugh, *Memoirs of the Affairs of Scotland from the Restoration of King Charles II*, 1821

Macphail, J. R. N., ed., *Papers Relating to the Macleans of Duart*, in Highland Papers vol. I, 1914

Macpherson, James, *Original Papers*, 1775

McCrie, T. M., ed., *Memoirs of William Veitch and George Bryson*, 1825

Orian Iain Luim, (ed.) A. M. Mackenzie, 1964

The New Statistical Account of Scotland, vol. VII, 1845

Nicoll, John, *A Diary of Public Transactions, 1650–1667*, 1836

Records of Argyll, compiled by Lord Archibald Campbell, 1885

The Register of the Privy Council of Scotland, second and third series, variously edited 1899–1933

Ruthven, Patrick Gordon of, *A Short Abridgement of Britane's Distemper*, 1844

Scottish Verse from the Dean of Lismore's Book, 1937

Steuart, A. F. ed., *Diary of Thomas Brown*, 1898

Thompson, E. M., ed., *Correspondence of the Family of Hatton*, vol. II, 1878

Wodrow, R., *Analecta*, vol. II, 1842

SECONDARY WORKS

Argyll: An Inventory of Ancient Monuments, vol. 7, 1992

Bevan, B., *James Duke of Monmouth*, 1973

Brown, A., *Memorials of Argyllshire*, 1889

Clarke, J. S., *The Life of James II*, 1816

Cowan, I. B., *The Scottish Covenanters, 1660–1688*, 1976

Cripps, D., *Elizabeth of the Sealed Knot*, 1975

Cunningham, A., *The Loyal Clans*, 1932

Ferguson, J., *Robert Ferguson the Plotter*, 1807

Fea, A., *King Monmouth*, 1902

Fox, C. J., *History of the Early Part of the Reign of James the Second*, 1808

Greaves, R. C., *Secrets of the Kingdom. British Radicals from the Popish Plot to the Revolution of 1688–1689*, 1992

Halley, K. H. D., *The First Earl of Shaftesbury*, 1968

Hewison, J.K., *The Covenanters*, vol. II, 1913

Hopkins, P., *Glencoe and the end of the Highland War*, 1986

Hopkirk, M., *Queen over the Water*, 1953

Hutton, R., *Charles II*, 1989

Kenyon, P., *The Popish Plot*, 1974

Lang, A, *Sir George Mackenzie, His Life and Times*, 1909

Lingard, J., *History of England*, vol. X, 1883

Macaulay, T. B. *History of England from the Accession of James II*, 1985

Mackenzie, W. C., *Andrew Fletcher of Saltoun*, 1935

McKerral, A., *Kintyre in the Seventeenth Century*, 1948

Macinnes, A. I., 'Repression and Conciliation: the Highland Dimension, 1660–1688', in *The Scottish Historical Review*, vol. 65, pp.167–95, 1986

Miller, J., *James II, A Study in Kingship*, 1977

Paterson, R. C., *A Land Afflicted Scotland and the Covenanter Wars, 1638–1690*, 1998

——, *Lords of the Isles. A History of Clan Donald*, 2001

Price, C., *Cold Caleb. The Scandalous Life of Ford Lord Grey First Earl of Tankerville*, 1956

Reid, J. *History of the County of Bute*, 1864

Stevenson, D., *Highland Warrior. Alasdair MacColla and the Civil Wars*, 1994

Willcock, J., *A Scots Earl in Covenanting Times*, 1907

Wodrow, R., *History of the Suffering of the Church of Scotland from the Restoration to the Revolution*, vols. III and IV, 1828–30

Index